T0194337

Yeah, What Else?

Yeah, What Else?

Essays, Memoirs, Poems, and Reviews

C.W. Spooner

iUniverse

YEAH, WHAT ELSE?
ESSAYS, MEMOIRS, POEMS, AND REVIEWS

iUniverse books may be ordered through booksellers or by contacting:

iUniverse
1663 Liberty Drive
Bloomington, IN 47403
www.iuniverse.com
1-800-Authors (1-800-288-4677)

ISBN: 978-1-4917-8943-8 (sc)
ISBN: 978-1-4917-9067-0 (e)

Library of Congress Control Number: 2016903026

Print information available on the last page.

iUniverse rev. date: 02/18/2016

This one is for Barbara
wife of forty years
loving mother of three
ace family photographer
multi-talented artist
settling beautifully into the role of Gigi

Also by the author:

'68—A Novel

Children of Vallejo—Collected Stories of a Lifetime

Contents

Introduction

The great comedian, Shelley Berman, used to do a routine in which he is talking on the phone to his girlfriend. Though we can only hear Shelley's side of the conversation, it becomes obvious that she is breaking up with him. He asks why, and she gives him a reason. He says, "Yeah, what else?" She gives him another reason. He says, "Yeah, what else?" And so it goes, through an endless list of reasons. With Berman's comic delivery and impeccable timing, it was hilarious.

Since the publication of my novel, *'68*, and my collection of short stories, *Children of Vallejo*, friends have been asking me what comes next. In effect, they are saying, "Yeah, what else?"

This ad hoc collection of essays, memoirs, poems, and reviews is my answer. It brings together many pieces that were originally published elsewhere, either on my blog, *The Rejected Writer's Journal*, or in the *Monday Update*, Harry Diavatis's fine weekly newsletter. Now they're all in one convenient place.

Cool, eh?

With this volume, I am done, complete, finished, *kaput*. You don't have to ask, "Yeah, what else?" anymore.

Well…maybe there'll be an occasional story…or a random poem… and I have ideas for a couple of novels. So go ahead and ask. And please keep on reading.

I.

Essays, Memoirs, and other scribblings...

"If you come to a fork in the road, take it."
-Yogi Berra

Shake Hands with Mr. Jolley

I couldn't wait for my dad to get home from work. He'd step off the bus at around 6:05 p.m. and boy, did I have something to show him that evening! Dario Lodigiani, Roy Nicely, and Frank "Lefty" O'Doul. Their baseball cards, that is.

I knew my dad would let lose a good laugh, especially over Lefty O'Doul. He loved old Lefty. And he loved the way Dario Lodigiani's name rolled off the tongue of the field announcer, pronouncing all five syllables of that surname. And how could you not cheer for a sweet-fielding shortstop named Roy Nicely?

It was the summer of 1950 and I would celebrate my eighth birthday later that year. We were great Pacific Coast League fans in those days. The PCL was our league, the "third major league" as we liked to think of it. The American and National leagues? They were way back east, inaccessible, out of reach. We knew that was where our great ballplayers went after we developed them here on the West Coast. Ping Bodie. Frankie Crosetti. The DiMaggio brothers. Ted Williams. But day in and day out, the PCL was our league and our team was the San Francisco Seals.

My friends and I would meet early each summer morning and head down the block and around the corner to Lenzi's Market on Georgia Street. There we'd wait for the bread truck driver to arrive, delivering fresh bread to stock Lenzi's shelves. I can't remember which brand it was, but one of the bakers attached PCL baseball cards to their loaves of bread. They weren't the same as the Topps major league cards; the card stock was lighter, the pictures sepia tone. But we collected them anyway, stashing them away with the intention of creating a scrapbook someday. We had established a friendship with the truck driver and learned that he always had a supply of lose cards in his cab. We'd be there waiting for him when he made his delivery. He'd engage us in a little banter and then slip us a few cards.

On this particular day, I couldn't believe my luck: Dario, Roy, and Lefty! My dad would get a kick out of this.

Dad came through the door, that old black lunchbox in hand, looking exhausted as usual. He washed up quickly then made his way to the dining room table. Mom joined him there to share a cold beer and chat about the day's happenings. She brought along a small juice glass, one that originally came packed with Kraft cheese spread, and poured me an inch or so of beer to share with them. It was our family ritual.

I showed Dad the three new baseball cards and, sure enough, his face lit up. He examined each one, turning it over to study the player's career statistics on the back. My dad was of the opinion that Lefty O'Doul was a fine manager and one of the great hitters of all time. And, Lefty was credited with popularizing baseball in Japan during the 1930s, and then again after World War II. He laughed and said that the Japanese revered old Lefty, referring to him as "Refty O'Dur San." I wasn't sure why that was funny, but it was good to hear my old man laugh.

I took the cards to my room and dropped them in an old shoebox. When I came back into the dining room, I could see that Mom and Dad were engaged in an intense conversation.

"Are you sure, Daddy?" she said.

"Yeah, Lou, I'm sure. It'll be fine."

I felt for a moment that I should leave the room and let them finish.

"Son," my dad said, beaming at me, "how would like to see a game at Seals Stadium?"

"Boy, would I!"

"Old Timers' Day is coming up in a few weeks. There'll be lots of great Seals veterans there, including a guy I played ball with growing up in Arkansas. His name is Smead Jolley. I'm gonna get tickets and we'll go see the game. How 'bout that?"

I couldn't believe it. I thought getting the baseball cards was a big deal. Now I was going to see these guys in the flesh, plus all the old timers, and this guy Smead Jolley. I found the calendar Mom kept in the kitchen and circled the date. It seemed so far away, I didn't think I could stand it.

———

We were up bright and early on the day of the game. My mom layed out my clothes for the day: sport coat, slacks, a dress shirt and tie. Hey, when you went to "The City," you dressed the part! The three of us looked like we were going to church rather than a ballgame.

It was a serious journey, traveling to San Francisco in those days. Our family didn't have a car at the time, relying instead on public transportation. We'd catch the Vallejo transit bus to the Greyhound station downtown, then a Greyhound express to the downtown terminal in S.F., and finally a Muni bus out to Seals Stadium at 16th and Bryant. Dad allowed about two and a half hours for this odyssey.

This was the era before Interstate 80 and the "big cut," when U.S. 40 crossed the Carquinez Bridge and swung to the west, following the shoreline through all the towns that rimmed the bay: Crockett, Rodeo, Hercules, Pinole, San Pablo, Richmond, Albany, Berkeley, and finally Emeryville and the majestic Bay Bridge into The City.

My parents let me sit next to the window where I could look out and monitor all the traffic on the bay: the fishing boats running out from Dowrellio's Resort in Crockett; freighters riding low in the water, bound for the C&H sugar refinery; oil tankers heading for that mile long pier poking out into the bay at Hercules; a Navy ship on its way to Mare Island for an overhaul; and then the massive grandstand at Golden Gate Fields race track and behind it, out on the bay, flocks of sailboats all around Alcatraz and Angel Island.

In those days, you had to be prepared for Emeryville. Most of the cities and towns along the shoreline dumped raw sewage into the bay, but the Emeryville Mudflats were notorious. If you rolled past when the tide was out, the stench could be overwhelming. My dad was ready. He had splashed a few drops of Mennen Skin Bracer on a clean white handkerchief and he handed it to me as we approached the mudflats so that I could cover my nose. Fortunately, the tide was high and I didn't really need it, but from that day on, I would associate the scent of Mennen Skin Bracer with Emeryville.

5

Seals Stadium opened in 1931 and was considered at the time to be one of the finest ballparks in the country, with its concrete grandstand, state-of-the-art lighting, and a modern public address system. Finally, we were there, walking up that broad ramp from Bryant Street and into the stadium. We followed the concourse around to the third base side, my dad checking the ticket stubs carefully, then up a stairway and out into the bright sunshine.

The sight of the manicured green field below us took by breath away. An army of groundskeepers was out on the field, dragging and raking and tamping and watering, fussing over a surface that already looked perfect to me. I thought it was the most beautiful sight I'd ever seen.

We found our seats behind the third base dugout and waited for the pre-game festivities to begin. My dad seemed a little nervous as we watched the men in vintage uniforms begin to emerge from the dugout.

"There he is, Lou, the big guy there." Dad pointed toward a large man wearing a home uniform that must have been white once upon a time. He hesitated a moment, then said, "Okay, I'm going down there." With that he slid out of our row and headed for the corner of the dugout.

"Why can't we go, Mom?"

"Just wait, honey. Let's see what happens."

My dad called to the large man and he ambled over to the railing. They spoke briefly and then a wide grin broke across the big man's face. He reached out his hand and my father shook it firmly. A second or two later, my dad motioned toward us to come on down and join them. We hurried to where the two men were standing and the adults exchanged introductions. Then my father turned to me and put his hand on my shoulder.

"Smead, this is Charles Jr. He wants to be a ballplayer when he grows up. Son, shake hands with Mr. Jolley."

I did as my father said, though I can't remember much of what came after that. I was riveted by the look on my old man's face and the pride in his voice. Mr. Jolley signed our program, we shook hands all around again, and then he left for the pre-game introductions.

I don't remember much about the game. I do remember that my dad was in a great mood all day, pointing out all the old timers, clapping loudly for Lefty O'Doul, and grinning at me when the field announcer intoned, "The batter…Dario Lod-i-gi-an-i." I remember that we had peanuts and hot dogs and chocolate malts. It was pretty much the best day ever.

When the game ended, we filed out of the stadium and rode the Muni back to the Greyhound station where we boarded the bus for the long ride home. Leaning against my mom, I was sound asleep before we crossed the Bay Bridge.

———

When I started to write this story, it occurred to me that after all these years Smead Jolley was just a name to me. I had no idea of his accomplishments in the game of baseball. Fortunately, in the age of Google, the answers are only a few clicks away.

Smead Jolley was born in Wesson, Arkansas, on January 14, 1902. He grew to be six feet four inches tall and two hundred and ten pounds and began his pro career as a pitcher. Much like Babe Ruth, he was too good of a hitter not to be an everyday player. He was soon moved to the outfield. The Seals sold his contract to the Chicago White Sox in 1930. He played for the White Sox and then the Boston Red Sox through the 1933 season, compiling a lifetime .305 batting average. After that, his contract was sold to the Hollywood Stars in the PCL and he moved back to the West Coast.

That seemed like a solid major league record. Why so short? A few more clicks of the mouse revealed that big Smead was considered one of the worst fielders that ever played the game. The story is told of his making three errors on one play. First, a ball went through his legs and caromed off the outfield wall. Then, as he turned around, it rolled through his legs again. Finally, he picked up the ball and threw it over the cutoff man. One play, three errors. Of course, there is no official scorecard or record of this game, and it is believed that a sportswriter concocted the tale to illustrate a point.

I knew there had to be more to the story, so I clicked the mouse a few more times and found Mr. Jolley's PCL record. Wow! He was a three-time batting champ in the Coast League, twice with the Seals (1927, 1928) and once (1938) with the Hollywood Stars and Oakland Oaks.

And then there was 1928. The Seals were league champs with an outfield composed of Jolley, Earl Averill, and Roy Johnson, and an infield that included Babe Pinelli, Frankie Crosetti, Ike Caveney, and Gus Suhr. Mr. Jolley compiled a .404 batting average, forty-five homeruns, and one hundred and eighty-eight runs batted in. He was a Triple Crown winner! He also scored one hundred and forty-three runs in what has to be one of the all-time great offensive seasons in professional baseball.

Smead Jolley was more than just a name.

———

So, what was it between my dad and Smead Jolley? Why the intense conversations and the concern prior to the meeting before the game? Was there a family feud—the Spooners and the Jolleys—like the Hatfields and McCoys? Was it a fight over a ballgame long ago? Maybe it was a dispute over a girl, a dark-haired beauty with flashing eyes that beguiled the two of them. After all, my dad was something of a bad boy as a young man. In the end, it didn't really matter because Smead Jolley obviously didn't hold a grudge.

Those old PCL baseball cards are long gone, as is the autographed program. What I managed to keep is the memory of my first trip to Seals Stadium and the look on my dad's face when he said, "Son, shake hands with Mr. Jolley."

Of Trains and Russell Street

A little nostalgia…

This is a story about trains, and especially about steam locomotives. My brief Wikipedia research tells me that steam engines began to be phased out in the early 1900's; however, they were still in commercial use into the early sixties. That said, I don't think America ever got over its romance with the age of steam.

For nearly thirty years, I worked in an office in downtown Roseville, California. Right across the street, just beyond a cyclone fence, was the Southern Pacific rail yard, one of the major switching centers on the West Coast. All day long, the diesel engines would hum around the yard, banging freight cars together, assembling trains that would head out to the world. Nobody paid much attention.

Ah, but when a steam locomotive came through town, that was another story.

As much as an hour beforehand, you would see people lining up along Atlantic Street, cameras slung around their necks, lawn chairs in tow. Before long they would be shoulder to shoulder with barely an open space along the fence. Then you'd hear the steam whistle, and you'd see the tall plume of gray smoke billowing into the air, and the locomotive would roll majestically into the yard. The engine would rest for a while, as though posing, while a thousand cameras clicked away. Finally, the whistle would sound again and she would roll away. And all the people would head for home.

This scene always reminded me of my childhood.

I was born in 1942 and grew up in a little two-bedroom house on Russell Street in Vallejo, California, just a block away from Steffan Manor School. It was a great neighborhood, full of fine families and lots of kids. My first best friend was Richard "Richie" Gunderson who lived just up the hill on Russell. For a long time it seemed that we were inseparable. We'd see each other almost every day and I don't remember ever being bored.

Cowboys and Indians was always a good pastime. We'd dress up in the full-on outfits—hats, vests, chaps, cap guns and holsters. We were

great fans of Roy Rogers and never missed his radio show featuring Dale Evans, Gabby Hayes, and that western chorus The Sons of the Pioneers. When we played, there was a lively competition to see which one of us would be Roy Rogers. That is until I saw a movie where the main character was a guy named Jim Banister. Jim could take on ten guys at a time, tie 'em all up and haul 'em away to the pokey. Wow! After that, Richie could be Roy anytime he wanted. *I* was Jim Banister.

The Gundersons had a big, open backyard and we would organize baseball games back there. Our teammates were drawn from all over the neighborhood, including Bobby Sather, Billy Sargent, the Waring brothers, and Bobbie Riddle. It didn't bother us that Bobbie was a girl. She was a good athlete and we were ahead of our time regarding equal opportunity.

Ah, but I digress. Remember…this story is about trains.

Richie's dear parents provided us with one of our all-time favorite things to do. On Sunday evenings when the weather was good, we'd jump in the Gundersons' sedan and head across the Carquinez Bridge—the old original structure— to watch the trains come and go at the Southern Pacific station in Crockett. I can't remember the make and model of the car, but in the forties, you had two features that were common in the backseat. First, there were armrests, like little shelves, on either side of the seat. They were just wide enough for a four- or five-year-old to park most of his butt. Nobody worried about car seats or seat belts in those days. Second, there were straps that hung down from the door posts, perfect for hanging on while you sat on the armrest.

It was always a battle to see who would sit on the right-hand side going toward Crockett. On that side, you had a perfect view of the *Golden Bear*, the merchant marine training ship docked at the Maritime Academy, as you went across the bridge. I can't remember how we decided this, whether it was by coin flip or drawing straws, but I remember it was always an issue. Of course there was nothing more disappointing than winning the right-hand side and finding that the *Golden Bear* was out to sea.

We'd sit out on the platform at the station waiting anxiously for a train to arrive. Mr. Gunderson had a pretty good handle on the train schedules and it seemed we never had to wait very long. In my memory, the sequence of events is always the same.

First, you'd see the baggage handlers start to roll the large flatbed carts out close to the tracks. Then you'd hear the steam whistle way down the tracks to the east as the train came through each crossing. Then you'd see that huge plume of smoke rising into the air, getting closer and closer. And then the train would pull into the station and the engine would roll slowly past us and come to a stop.

The scene would become a beehive of activity then. The porters would jump down and drop their wooden step stools, a few passengers would get off, the baggage carts would fill up, new passengers would come out to board, their baggage would be loaded—all in a matter of a few minutes.

We'd always wait until the conductor stood on the step of one of the cars, swung his lantern and shouted "All aboard!" Then CHUG chug chug, CHUG chug chug, CLANG clang clang, as the mighty engine began to gain traction and all the couplings engaged, the train would roll out of the station and on down along the rim of the bay toward Oakland.

I said this story was about trains and steam locomotives, but that wasn't true. It's really about memories and friendships that are an important part of your life, the kind that stay warm and gentle on your mind more than sixty-five years later.

Thanks for the memories, Richie.

The Rites of Spring

"I got the best shit in town. Nobody's got shit like I got shit. I tell you, it's the best shit in town."

He was a wiry little man with a thick salt-and-pepper moustache and he wore bib overalls and a railroad cap. He spoke with a heavy accent, which my mom identified as German. His dump truck looked like it was built by hand on a very old Ford chassis. The mechanism that lifted the bed was a jerry-rigged cog and chain contraption that he cranked by hand, and the sides of the bed were made of two-by-fours and plywood. Onto this strange looking rig, he could load ten yards of steer manure, which he delivered to our house on Russell Street every spring.

The delivery generally took place on a weekday when my dad was at work, so my mom took care of having the load dumped in our driveway and paying the man for his goods. Mom loved to tell the story and I always thought she was exaggerating. That is until I witnessed it several times when I was home on spring break. That gentleman really could go on a five-minute rant about "...the best shit in town."

My dad's vegetable garden was his pride and joy. He was an Arkansas farm boy and I suspect that gardening put him in touch with his roots. We had a narrow strip of grass that ran along the back of the house, ten feet wide at the most, then the rest of the yard—maybe fifty by sixty feet—was given over to vegetables. Dad raised several varieties of lettuce, squash, and beans. There were root crops like carrots, radishes, and turnips. He also raised Swiss chard which was one of my favorites. But without question, he poured the greatest measure of his love and labor into his prized sweet corn.

Dad favored a hybrid variety of corn called Golden Bantam. Over the years, he experimented with others, but always came back to that one variety. He would plant a couple of long rows, let it get well up out of the ground—maybe six or eight inches—then plant another couple of rows, and so on. The happy outcome was that we'd have sweet corn ripening and ready for the table all summer long. It was the staple of our summer diet: whatever else was going on the table, it would land there next to the sweet corn.

I have to admit that this turned me into a sweet corn snob. My dad taught me that when corn is picked, the sugar in the kernels begins to convert into starch. If it sits around for a while, that wonderful sweetness is lost, and all the butter and salt in the world will not make up for it. I rarely buy corn at the supermarket because I know it just won't measure up.

So, the wiry little German man would deliver ten yards of steer manure to our driveway and that weekend, my dad would begin the process of carting it back to his garden plot, one wheelbarrow load at a time. He'd spread it out over the fallow ground and then begin digging it into the soil by hand, a process that would take most of a Saturday or Sunday afternoon. He'd stop every now and then for a cold beer, or to scoop up one of our cats and scratch its ears, but he'd always finish the job by sundown. A shovel was the only tool he needed. Dad was past his sixtieth birthday when we finally convinced him to hire someone with a rototiller to do the job.

Why am I telling you all this? Well, it's almost time to head over to my favorite garden supply store and load the trunk of my Honda with eight or ten bags of steer manure. This I will spread on my four-by-twelve foot tomato patch and then dig it into the soil with my trusty shovel. It doesn't take more than an hour or so, but I'll manage to stop for a couple of beers. And my beloved cat, Sophie, will be hanging around, keeping an eye on the proceedings. Maybe this is all a guy really needs: a piece of God's good earth, a sturdy shovel, a loyal cat, and a couple of beers chilling in the fridge.

I've had good production from several varieties—Early Girl, Better Boy, Sweet 100, to name a few—but my all-time champ is the Lemon Boy, a nice big yellow tomato. Good old Lemon Boy just seems to love my little piece of ground.

Here's a little bit of irony: for all my dad's expertise and hard work, he could never grow a decent tomato. Maybe he just overwhelmed them with care. They always seemed to turn out with thick white cores and they were virtually tasteless. One summer, our neighbors, the MacLaughlins, drove to Oklahoma to visit family. They planted some tomatoes before they left and told my dad that if he watered them, he was welcome to whatever fruit developed. These poor neglected plants—unstaked, untended, unloved—produced the biggest and best tasting tomatoes ever grown in Vallejo.

My dad swore he'd never plant another vine, which leads me to wonder if he would have admired my tomatoes as much as I admired his corn. It's something to ponder.

At any rate, in a week or so I'll make my annual trek to the garden shop and load the trunk with bags of steer manure. I can't say it's the best shit in town, but my Lemon Boy sure seems to like it.

Color It Notorious

"Lower Georgia." Okay, now close your eyes and say it again: "Lower Georgia."

The very name evokes indelible images for those of us who grew up in Vallejo in the forties and fifties. It was the area of town that was periodically overrun by sailors, and watched closely by the Shore Patrol with their white helmets and shiny black nightsticks. It was that eclectic collection of shops, cafes, bars, flophouses, and brothels, all poised to service the Pacific Fleet. It was the place your parents warned you about, as in "Don't ever let me catch you down there."

We had a slightly different point of view in our household. My father was a twenty-year Navy man and he'd seen ports of call all around the world. In his view, Vallejo was a typical Navy town and Lower Georgia was just another colorful neighborhood.

Neighborhoods, whether plain or colorful, are anchored by their institutions, and Lower Georgia was no different in that respect. In fact, our family did regular business with several of those institutions, beginning with the Skipper's Club located at the foot of Georgia Street. Technically you could say that Skipper's wasn't a part of Lower Georgia, but it was certainly the gateway. It was also my dad's favorite place to cash his paycheck from the shipyard. I go with him on the check cashing expedition because nobody thought twice in those days about a little guy tagging along to his dad's favorite saloon. While my dad had a beer with his friends, I'd hang around outside on the dock watching the water taxis race back and forth across the Mare Island Strait, taking the workers to the shipyard and bringing sailors ashore on liberty. Many passengers would stop off at Skipper's for a cold one before heading into town, and I'm sure quite a few visited the men's room with the famous sign over the toilet: "We aim to please. You aim too please."

Further up Georgia Street was another venerable establishment: Parmisano & Sons Fish Market, marked by that well-known sign in the shape of a fish. Parmisanos' had the best fresh seafood in town. It was a narrow storefront that extended deep into the building, and on the right as you came in there was a long tiled counter where the catch-of-the-day was displayed on a bed of ice. Depending on the season, you would see black and red snapper, cod, halibut, sole, salmon, crab, clams, oysters, or all of the above. We weren't Catholic, but my parents chose to observe that old custom of eating fish on Friday. Mom would shop at Parmisanos' every week to buy a nice salmon steak for my dad, and some halibut or other white fish for the rest of the family.

The Parmisanos were also known for their oyster stew, which they prepared and put up in quart jars. It was like New England clam chowder with oysters instead of clams, and it was my dad's favorite Saturday lunch. I'd try a little of the broth, but I couldn't bring myself to sample the oysters.

As my buddies and I got a little older and took up fishing around the bay, Parmisanos' was always our first stop to buy bait. They had fresh sardines, trucked in from San Francisco, or maybe all the way from Monterey. These sardines were big and plump, just right to be filleted for bait to entice a striped bass. The bait counter was way in the back of the store and watching the packaging process was almost as much fun as the fishing that followed. It went something like this: weigh out several pounds of sardines; grab a shoebox from a stack against the wall; throw in a generous scoop of sawdust; toss the sardines on top of the sawdust bed; take an equally generous scoop of shaved ice and toss it on top of the sardines; put the top on the shoebox and wrap it in newspaper; tie up the package in sturdy twine. And there you had it: your bait for the day wrapped in the *Times-Herald*, bound up in a neat little package to go.

You could have blindfolded me and walked me into Parmisanos' and I would know exactly where I was. There is nothing quite like the smell of fresh fish on ice, or fresh sardines on a bed of sawdust.

My dad loved professional wrestling, which took us to another institution down on Georgia Street: the Farragut Club. As you came in from the street, there was a wide staircase that took you up a couple of flights of stairs to the second floor. There you entered the arena with a boxing/wrestling ring in the center, surrounded by tiered seating that reached up toward the rafters. My guess is that the arena could seat about a thousand people. The whole place appeared to be constructed of wood, and more than once the thought crossed my mind that it would only take one match to set the whole place aflame.

The Farragut was a regular stop on the pro wrestling circuit in Northern California and I loved going there with my dad. I can't remember many of the names from that era, but my favorites were Mike and Ben Sharp, "The Sharp Brothers." They were a great tag team. Another favorite was Leo "The Lion" Nomellini, the Hall of Fame tackle for the San Francisco Forty-Niners. Leo supplemented his NFL paycheck by wrestling in the off-season, usually playing the role of the good guy.

There was one other wrestler that I will never forget: Antonio "Argentina" Rocca. In the late forties and early fifties, he was the hottest star in pro wrestling. He wrestled barefoot and reportedly did amazing things with his feet, almost as if they were a second pair of hands. When my dad heard he was coming to Vallejo, he bought tickets as soon as they went on sale.

The arena was jammed the night of Rocca's appearance. After the preliminary matches, when he finally came down into the ring, the crowd gave him a rousing welcome. The match started poorly for our hero. The bad guy pulled some nasty and illegal tricks and suddenly, Antonio was stunned. Then came a clothesline tackle with the bad guy flying off the ropes, then a slam and another slam, and within the first five minutes, Antonio was nearly pinned—twice! He managed to kick out, but only at the last instant. Then the bad guy got into an argument with the referee, which gave Antonio time to clear his head. And then he pounced like a jungle cat. What an attack! He was tumbling and flying all over the ring, doing magical things with those amazing feet, and before long the bad guy was in big trouble. Then a slam, and another slam, followed by an airplane slam, and Antonio was on top of the bad guy and the referee was counting—1-2-3—and it was over. The crowd went crazy! I'd seen a lot of matches at the Farragut Club, but I'd never seen anything like that.

We filed out of the arena, down that broad staircase and out onto Georgia Street, and then up to the bus stop for the ride back to Steffan Manor. My dad was in a great mood. "Well, Bub," he said, "I think we got our money's worth tonight."

My father liked to tell stories of his Navy days, when he and his shipmates would hit town and go honky-tonkin'. Now, a honky-tonk by my dad's definition was a good bar with live music and a dance floor, a place where the sailors could rub up against the townsfolk to their mutual advantage. After listening to these stories for a number of years, my mom finally asked my dad to take her honky-tonkin'. So, in the late-forties equivalent of a date night, they left me with my older brother and sister and headed for Lower Georgia and some places my father was familiar with.

They were on their second or third stop, having a fine time, when my dad said, "Lou, see that woman sitting over there at the bar?" Mom said she looked up to see "…a blonde dame wearing a trench coat." Dad said, "What do you think she's wearing under that coat?" Then the dame shifted on the stool, the coat opened slightly and the answer was revealed: nothing, nothing at all. "Oymygawd, Daddy, get me out of here!" My mom grabbed my dad's arm and pulled him out onto the street where they hailed a taxi for the ride home. Mom never again asked to go honky-tonkin', but she loved telling the story. And it got a little better each time I heard it.

My cousin Eldon was a thirty-year Navy veteran. One day I told him the story of Mom and Dad's honky-tonk adventure. He laughed, but then he grew very serious. He assured me that Lower Georgia was notorious throughout the Pacific Fleet. Every sailor knew of our town and its special enterprise zone. If memory serves, his exact words were, "You could buy or sell anything there, Charlie." It took a while for the many implications of that statement to sink in.

Which brings us back to the original question: was Lower Georgia that dangerous, notorious place your parents warned you about? Or was it simply a colorful neighborhood, anchored by enduring institutions and possessing a certain faded beauty?

I prefer the colorful neighborhood option. Though I have to admit, if I was raising my kids in Vallejo during the forties and fifties, they would hear from me in no uncertain terms: "Don't you *ever* let me catch you *down there.*"

Who'd You Get Today?

"Who'd you get today?" That was the standard summer greeting when you saw your buddies. Not, "What's up?" or "How's it goin'?" Simply, "Who'd you get today?"

It referred to our summertime hobby during the mid- to late-fifties, which was collecting autographed pictures of Major League baseball players. The way it worked was this: we would walk up to the branch post office on the frontage road along Highway 40 and buy a stack of two-cent postcards. Then we would hunker down and write cards to all of our favorite players, addressed to the stadium in the city where they played. For example:

> *To: Mickey Mantle*
> *C/O The New York Yankees*
> *Yankee Stadium*
> *The Bronx, New York*

> *Dear Mickey:*
> *You are my favorite player and I am a big fan of the Yankees. Please send me an autographed picture of yourself. I hope you win the triple crown this year, and that the Yankees win the pennant.*

Off in the mail would go fifty to one hundred postcards at a time. And then we would wait every morning for the mail to arrive. Sure enough, within a week or so, back would come the requested product in the form of a picture postcard. If you were lucky, the postcard would be autographed personally by the player. In many cases, the autographs were preprinted on the card. It was a never-ending quest because each year the teams would prepare a new set of postcards, so you were constantly trying to get the current year's edition.

There were several challenges to overcome. First, some players seemed impossible to get. These, of course, were some of the game's great stars who I'm sure realized that their pictures and autographs had significant value to collectors. I don't think I was ever successful in getting Stan "The Man" Musial, though some of my friends actually made that catch.

Second, there was the problem of the preprinted autograph. We got around that by writing letters to the players and enclosing a self-addressed postcard:

> *Dear Mr. Ted Williams:*
> *I think you are the greatest hitter of all time. Please autograph the enclosed self-addressed postcard and mail it to me. I hope you hit .400 this year.*

You might ask what was the genesis of this little hobby? If memory serves, the credit goes to Bobby Morenco, one of my friends from Little League. I believe he was the original collector. Don Decious, who lived across the street from me, was also an avid and innovative collector. He went so far as to create scrapbooks with all the cards and autographs mounted neatly, preserved for posterity. I had a mediocre collection, but I was in the game, as least enough to shout out the standard greeting to my friends throughout the summer months: "Who'd you get today?"

Then came 1956, the year of The Great Hall of Fame Breakthrough. Somehow, someone—was it Morenco or Decious?—obtained a list of the mailing addresses for all living Hall of Fame members. Wow! Out went the letters with self-addressed postcards enclosed:

> *Dear Mr. Ty Cobb:*
> *I think you are the greatest hitter of all time. I hope your record stands forever. Please autograph the enclosed postcard and mail it to me.*

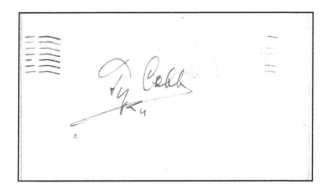

And back they came, those priceless postcards, autographed by the likes of Carl Hubbell, Frankie Frisch, Rogers Hornsby, Bill Dickey, Jimmy Foxx, Mel Ott, Ty Cobb, and Joe DiMaggio, to name just a few. I couldn't believe it. Ty Cobb held my postcard in his hands and signed it with a bright green marking pen! Joltin' Joe, The Yankee Clipper, actually wrote a few words on my card: "Best Wishes from Joe DiMaggio." I'm in my seventies now and I still get chills every time I hold those cards.

As I said, my collection wasn't much. It certainly couldn't compare to Don or Bobby's. Along about 1959, I began to lose interest. My cards were bound with a rubber band and stored away in an old shoebox. Later, I gave them to my then-brother-in-law, Rick Beaver. Years later, he returned them to me, which was a very thoughtful thing to do. When my sons reached Little League age along about 1987, I found the old cards and shared the history with them. Now the cards are back in that shoebox waiting for me to do what I should have done many years ago: mount them properly in a scrapbook and make sure they are passed along to future generations.

That scrapbook is definitely on my "to do" list, along with several other things. But my list is notorious as the place where projects go to die. At least I got as far as sharing the story with all of you.

It's funny, but I can still hear my buddies calling just like it was yesterday: "Hey Charlie, who'd you get today?"

PS: I finally got the cards mounted in a scrapbook. Check that one off the "to do" list.

Tody

I was thumbing through some old yearbooks the other day and I came across this inscription in the 1957 Hogan Junior High Totem Pole, written by my friend Tony Petrillo:

> *Chawie,*
>   *It's been a lot of fun to be around you this year. We can have a real ball this summer. Maybe one of these days, we can rob Sperry's by the way of our secret entrance. (ha ha)*
>   *Your iddy biddy buddy,*
>   *Tody*

That entry brought back a flood of memories. First, let me explain the "Chawie" and the "Tody." I don't know how this got started, but Tony always called me Chawie, and I always called him Tody (pronounced TOAD-ee). We shared some pretty remarkable adventures and he's a guy that, in the words of the old song, will always be "gentle on my mind."

Tony was a lot of fun to hang around with. He became a close friend of Dillon Mini, and Dillon and I were like brothers. Tony had a way about him that kept me in stitches most of the time. When he was around, the laughter went on nonstop. As we got older, into our high school years, we started to lose touch with Tony. He got a job very early on, working for a supermarket chain, and he was an incredibly hard worker. And so, we began to see less and less of him. I do remember that he purchased a beautiful mid-fifties Buick that we would go cruising in from time to time. I picture it to be much like that Buick in *Rain Man*, except that it was a hardtop rather than a convertible.

But, I digress. Let me explain that reference to Sperry's (i.e., Sperry Mills).

One of our favorite things to do was to grab our well-maintained tackle and head for one of the many fishing spots in the waters around Vallejo, including places like Dillon's Point, Glen Cove, The Lighthouse, Lemon Street Pier, Ryder Street, and The Old Destroyer. We caught a lot of flounder and the occasional striped bass, but mostly we just logged a lot of memories about time well spent with great friends.

There was a legend, widely accepted as true, that the best place to fish for striped bass was from the concrete wall at Sperry Mills. I think we can credit our friend Jerry Warren for keeping this legend alive, because his dad, his grandfather, and his uncle all worked at Sperry's. The story went like this: when ships came in to unload sacks of grain at the mill, the spilled grain that was left over was scooped up and tossed into the Mare Island Strait, right off the concrete wall that faced the southern end of Mare Island. Allegedly, striped bass were fond of this dumped grain, and so they would school just off the wall to feed, making them easy pickings for eager fishermen. I can't honestly tell you that striped bass like their Wheaties, but that's how the legend was told.

I ask you: how could a boy resist a challenge like that?

At the crack of dawn one Sunday morning in the spring of 1957, my mom dropped us off—Tony, Dillon, and me—at the Lemon Street Pier. We had stopped at Parmisanos' Fish Market to buy bait and our cover story was that we would be at the pier all morning and into the early afternoon, at which time Mom would come to pick us up. As soon as she drove out of sight, we headed south along the railroad tracks, away from good old Lemon Street and toward the front gate of Sperry Mills. We had been told that there was a hole in the fence surrounding the Sperry plant, somewhere up on the hill in the northeast corner of the property. Our plan was to find that hole, make our way to the legendary wall and catch limits of grain-fed striped bass.

On a quiet Sunday morning, what could possibly go wrong?

The hole was right where we were told, in the northeast corner of the cyclone fence. No sooner had we crawled through and started down the hill, than a car came screeching to a halt on the road just beyond a large building. The driver of the car yelled at us to halt, which we took as a signal to take off running down the hill and south along the building. Before we could reach the corner of the structure, the car came flying around in front of us. The driver jumped out and again ordered us to halt. At this point, we gave up. It was obvious our fishing plans had been cancelled. After a few stern words about trespassing and criminal penalties, the man loaded us into the car and drove us to the front gate.

I think we kind of got to him though, because on the way to the gate, he told us a great fish story.

It seems there was a Chinese gentleman who often fished from the wall in front of the mill. One day, he hooked what appeared to be a huge fish. He played the fish carefully and relentlessly for more than four hours. Finally, it came into sight. It was a sturgeon, about eight feet long and weighing at least three hundred pounds. The Chinese gentleman played the fish right up to the wall and directed a companion to get a gaff into the monster. As they attempted to gaff the fish, it shook its mighty head and threw the hook. And then it slowly swam away.

What a story! As we walked away, heading back toward the Lemon Street Pier, we swore that we'd be back.

Another activity that we enjoyed during the summer was to hike out to the East Vallejo Little League field, out on Benicia Road by the Auto Movies, to take batting practice. The permanent fence at EVLL was about two hundred and eighty feet away, and it was a lot of fun to see how many you could hit out of the park. After a couple of hours of BP, we'd go over to the Auto Movies, find (or create) a hole in the fence, and let ourselves in to mess around on the playground down in front of the screen. This drove the security guard nuts! He would come driving down in his pickup truck, pitching and bucking over the terraced rows, to chase us out. After a couple of summers of this, he was getting pretty frustrated. One day he chased Tony, Dillon, and me out through the fence, but he wasn't through. He sped back to the front gate and came roaring around to the ballpark, determined to apprehend us and put a stop to our shenanigans.

We saw him coming and ran out into the field adjacent to the park to hide in the tall grass. The grass had to be at least three feet high and we were sure that he wouldn't follow us out there. Wrong! He headed his old beat-up pickup out into the field, coming straight toward us. We jumped up and took off running, finally making it to a row of houses that bordered the field. We jumped the back fence of a particular house and started to run through and out onto the residential street.

Tony didn't see the twisted wire clothesline. It caught him across the upper lip on the left side of his face and left a deep gash—and more blood than I'd ever seen in my life. I don't remember much after that.

I know we got Tony home and from there, his parents took him to the hospital for stitches. And that's how Tony got that scar on his lip. If anything, it only added to his Italian good looks.

I think it was the summer of 1959 when Tony, Dillon, and I decided to go up to Tahoe, to the cabin Dillon's parents owned near the South Tahoe Y, and go trout fishing on the Upper Truckee River. Tony had never done any stream fishing and we were determined to show him how. Dillon and I came prepared with our usual stream fishing outfits: T-shirts, old gym shorts, and beat-up Chuck Taylor high-tops. We could go wading in the stream to our hearts content. Tony forgot to bring shorts, so he decided to take a pair of jeans and cut them off. We looked around the Minis' cabin but could not find a pair of scissors, so Tony took a butcher knife and set about cutting off his jeans. You can probably tell what's coming. The knife slipped and Tony put a deep gash in that tender spot between the thumb and forefinger on his left hand. There was more blood than I had seen since the clothesline incident.

We should have hauled him off to an emergency room to get stitched up, but Tony wouldn't hear of it. We found some gauze pads and adhesive tape and patched him up as best we could, and the next morning, we went fishing. I wish I could say that we caught limits of beautiful rainbow trout, but the fact is the fishing was lousy.

Tony did the best he could with a huge bandage on his left hand.

The last time I saw Tony was in the summer of 1969, though he didn't see me. I was living in Alameda at the time, and on the spur of the moment one evening, I hustled out to the Oakland Coliseum to catch an A's game. I was lucky to get a seat in the lower level of the grandstand behind the first base dugout. The game was close with the A's leading by a run or two in ninth inning. I happened to look down toward the box seats and saw a couple making their way up to the concourse, apparently intending to beat the rush when the game ended. The girl was gorgeous, with beautiful platinum-colored hair. I looked at the guy with her and realized it was Tony. They stopped at the concourse level and knelt down to catch the final out of the game. I yelled, "Hey, Tony," but he couldn't hear me over the noise of the crowd. So I started to scoot my way out of the row to try to get to them and say hello. Just then, the game ended and the rush for the exits was on. I lost them in the crowd.

I think back to Tony's entry in my '57 Totem Pole, and I wish I could write a short note to him. It would go something like this:

> *Dear Tody:*
>
> *I'm sorry I couldn't catch up with you at that A's game back in 1969. It would have been great to visit with you and get caught up with everything going on in your life, and it would have been nice to meet that beautiful girl you were with. (ha ha)*
>
> *I know our friendship left its mark (scars?) on you, and I feel like I owe you an apology. But we did have some great adventures, didn't we? You're one of those guys I'll always remember fondly. Here's wishing you all the best.*
>
> *Your iddy biddy buddy,*
> *Chawie*

Delivery Boy Blues

The engine began to sputter and cough and cut out, then surge again. I looked at the gas gauge and my eyes nearly popped out of my head. It wasn't just on empty; the needle was below the "E," resting on that little metal peg on the far end of the arc. After a few more coughs and spurts, there was dead silence as I steered the tiny BMW Isetta off to the side of the road, flat out of gas.

"Oh no! You idiot!" I yelled. "How could you not check the gas gauge?"

This was it, the final straw, a clear-cut firing offense. But wait a minute. What was that down the road about a quarter mile? It was a gas station with the lights burning brightly. Maybe, just maybe, I could still salvage this situation. I popped open the door and jumped out, slammed it hard and locked it carefully, and took off on an all-out sprint toward the lights of the station.

I was beginning my senior year at Vallejo High School, and my after school and Saturday job was to be the official delivery boy for Wessel's Pharmacy. My ball-playing friends, Frank Bodie and Joey Butler, had worked for the Wessels, but they had graduated and were heading off to college. When I heard about the opening, I applied for the job right away. This was considered a plum position, especially when you considered that you got to zip all around town in the Isetta, affectionately known as the "Drug Bug." The Wessels used it prominently in their advertising: order your prescriptions from Wessel's and the Drug Bug will bring them right to your door.

Wessel's Pharmacy was located about a block east of the El Rey Theater at the corner of Tennessee and Monterey streets. It was a pleasant storefront on the south side of Tennessee. There were rows of shelves filled with cosmetics and health aids and sundries as you came into the store, and the pharmacy counter was in the rear. Bud and Thelma Wessel were the owner-operators and, except for the delivery boy, were the only employees. If memory serves, the Wessels were only in their fifties, but the hard pace was beginning to take its toll. I heard that they were in financial trouble but determined to overcome the situation by sheer hard work. They were there to open the store in the morning, and they were there an hour or so after the 9:00 p.m. closing time, six days a week. And they were exhausted.

There is a story about Mrs. Wessel convincing her husband to take an evening off and go home to get some rest. When he left, he forgot something important that he intended to take home, so Mrs. W sent the delivery boy (probably Frank or Joey) to take it to him. When he arrived, there was Mr. Wessel parked in the driveway, sound asleep behind the wheel. He couldn't even make it into the house.

Thelma Wessel was a short, heavy-set woman with a very sweet disposition. She smiled and laughed easily and it was easy to like her. Bud Wessel was another story. He was tall and slim with gray hair that was rapidly going white. He wore reading glasses that tended to slide down his nose and when he looked at you, he would drop his chin so that he could gaze over those glasses. That gaze could be withering when he was angry, but occasionally, you could get a smile and a laugh and his eyes would twinkle. He truly looked the part of the wise and trusted pharmacist.

I think it was Joey who warned me that Mr. Wessel was not easy to get along with. I was so happy to have the job that I paid little attention to that warning. My mom saw to it that I received an allowance every week and when I started working, we kept that arrangement. I just endorsed my paycheck from Wessel's and gave it to her. It really wasn't much, but it made me feel good to think that I was helping out.

Mr. W and I never really hit it off, mainly because I couldn't seem to do anything right. When I got to the store after school, there were generally a half dozen prescriptions to be delivered, and my primary duty was to get organized and plan the route carefully, minimizing travel time and the distance between stops. There were maps available to assist in this task and, after all, I'd grown up in Vallejo. I thought I knew my way around. Somehow I just couldn't get it right. I managed to get lost frequently and always took too long to complete my deliveries, at least in the eyes of Mr. Wessel.

Mrs. Wessel would occasionally give me a short list of items to pick up at the market when I was out. If she gave me five items, I usually managed to get at least two of them wrong. Three-for-five is good in baseball, but not so hot on a trip to the market.

On slow nights, they would give me busy work to do, jobs like dusting the bottles of medicine on the shelves in the pharmacy. I couldn't even seem to do that correctly, prompting Mr. Wessel to patiently explain once again what he expected. I'd march in every day determined to do better, but the harder I tried, the worse it seemed to get.

Simply put, I had become a perpetual screw-up.

The biggest source of tension between Mr. Wessel and me was the Drug Bug. He loved that little Isetta beyond all understanding. It was his baby. It was a temperamental little beast and I never quite got the hang of it. When it had been sitting for an extended period of time, there was a strict sequence of steps you had to follow before you turned the key to engage the starter. If you didn't execute the sequence precisely, the bug would backfire. That tiny vehicle could produce a cannon blast that was truly amazing. I seldom ever got it right. The Isetta would backfire and as I chugged off down the street, Mr. Wessel would pop his head out the side door of the building and glare at me over his glasses.

And now there I was, running as hard as I could for the bright lights of the service station, desperately trying to recover from yet another mistake. I raced onto the lot and headed for the small office next to the service bay. Suddenly a huge grin broke across my face. Sitting in the office was my friend Frankie Arellano. I was so glad to see him, I could have kissed him right there.

"Frank! I didn't know you worked here."

"Hi, Charlie. What's up?"

"I ran out of gas down the road. I'm out delivering prescriptions for Wessel's. Can I get a can of gas—fast?"

"Sure, I've got a can right here."

In a matter of minutes, I was sprinting back toward the Drug Bug, the gas can banging against my leg. I dumped the gas into the tank, jumped in and turned the key. The little Isetta backfired happily as the engine sprang to life. I made a quick stop at the station to return the can.

"How much do I owe you, Frankie?"

"Forget it. It's on the house."

"Thanks, buddy. You're saving my life."

With that, I was back on the road. The whole episode cost me no more than twenty minutes. On the way back to the pharmacy after my deliveries, I decided that if Frank and I were the only people in the world who ever knew about this little adventure that would be just fine.

A few days later, I showed up for work to find Mr. Wessel sitting at the counter in the back of the store with a ledger book open in front of him. He was in a great mood and actually smiled at me as I came in. It seems he kept a detailed record of the Isetta's performance and there had been a miraculous spike in the miles per gallon. He showed me the numbers and said, "Isn't that amazing? How could that happen?" He was ecstatic. I felt my stomach drop as I realized that it was my "free" gallon of gas that had skewed the numbers. Frankie didn't charge me for it, so I didn't enter it in the delivery log. I didn't know Mr. W tracked every detail with such precision. I just shrugged and went about planning my afternoon deliveries.

Years later when I would tell this story, I would say that Mr. Wessel was so happy, I didn't have the heart to tell him what really happened. The truth is I didn't have the guts to admit to another compound screw-up.

It wasn't too long after that when things came to a head. I came into work on Saturday morning, received my paycheck from Mrs. Wessel, and set about doing odd jobs until some prescriptions were ready for delivery. Once again, I wasn't performing the tasks to Bud Wessel's satisfaction. He launched into a very calm, quiet, patient lecture about how he wanted things done. He might as well have been screaming in my face. I snapped. I couldn't take anymore.

"That's it," I said. "Nothing I do is good enough for you. I quit!" With that I stormed toward the door.

"You know," he said very calmly, "you got paid for today. It's included in your check."

I stopped dead in my tracks and turned around. I had no clue what to do at that point. I was utterly destroyed, no longer the abused worker standing up for my dignity and self-respect, just a humiliated kid without a leg to stand on. I took a tentative step back into the store, deciding lamely that I'd have to finish out that day on the job.

"No," Mr. Wessel said, "that's okay. It's probably better if you go."

I headed for home, wiping my eyes on my sleeve, trying to decide how to tell my mom that I'd quit my job and why. My "career" with Wessel's Pharmacy had lasted just a couple of months.

Mr. Wessel did an interesting thing after I quit. He wrote a letter to my mom. It arrived in the mail a few days later. He wrote that he was sure I was a fine, intelligent young man with a bright future. He was sorry that things had not worked out, but he wished only the best for me and our entire family. It was a kind and generous thing to do and I felt my anger toward him begin to melt away.

It couldn't have been more than a couple of years later that I heard Bud Wessel had died. I knew exactly what had happened: he'd finally worked himself to death. I felt a heavy sadness for him and for Mrs. Wessel too.

Hopefully we learn something as we live through these experiences. So, what are the lessons learned from all of this? Don't put extra pressure on yourself, because it won't make you a diamond. Work hard and do the best you can, but don't take it home with you. Don't think you need to have all the answers, and if you are struggling, reach out for help.

That's a pretty good list for starters. It's great if you are smart and lucky and you only have to learn these lessons once. If smart and lucky aren't your things, well then, you get to learn them over and over again.

More than five decades later, I'm only sure of one thing: I still owe Frankie Arellano for that gallon of gas.

A Place Nobody Ever Heard Of

"Ohmygawd!" Danny came barging into my room clutching a copy of the *Minneapolis Tribune*. "Did you see this? Johnny Cash is going to be at the St. Paul Auditorium tomorrow night. Johnny Cash!"

"Oh yeah?" I replied. That's about all the enthusiasm I could muster. I liked Johnny Cash well enough. I was just not a big fan of country music. Now if he'd said Miles Davis or Dave Brubeck, then I'd have responded with an *Ohmygawd* of my own.

"Oh, man, it's tomorrow night," Danny continued. "I've got to find a way to get there. Where the heck is the St. Paul Auditorium anyway?"

"I think it's in St. Paul," I cracked. I couldn't resist the set-up. "You know, Orville has a car. Maybe you can talk him into going."

Danny brightened at that prospect and hurried off to find Orville.

It was late March of 1962 and I was in Minneapolis to attend Gale Institute, a trade school that promised to train me for "…a high-paying job in the airline industry." I had completed the correspondence portion of the Gale program over a period of several months, and was just beginning the four-week residence course. There were four of us living at Mrs. Olsen's boardinghouse, just around the corner from the school in the Hennepin-Lake district. It was a large two-story home with a couple of bedrooms upstairs that we shared, and it had a full basement that had been converted into a kitchen. There we could store all the staples of bachelor survival: frozen dinners, peanut butter and jelly, milk, and the essential bag of Oreo cookies.

My housemates were an eclectic bunch. Jerry, my roommate, was from Waverly, Iowa, and was simply a great guy, full of mischief and laughter. I swear I could have picked him up out of his family's farm in Iowa, set him down in the neighborhood where I grew up, and he would fit right in.

Danny was from Waterloo, Iowa, and though he was a good guy, we didn't quite click. Maybe it was because (with apologies to Donnie and Marie) he was a little bit country and I was a little bit jazz. More likely it was because he enjoyed taking shots at my hometown. He'd never heard of Vallejo, California, and he was sure nobody else ever heard of it either. I told him all about our rich heritage and our contributions to the U.S. Navy via Mare Island Naval Shipyard. And I pointed out that Waterloo wasn't exactly The Big Apple. None of that slowed him down a bit. Needless to say, I was glad that Jerry was my roommate.

Orville, Danny's roommate, was from somewhere in Ohio. I'm not sure he ever told us where. He was older than the rest of us, mid-twenties I believe, and painfully shy. It was hard to get a word out of him. We'd prod him and needle him a little, trying to get him to loosen up, but it was no use. We couldn't get him to react. Oh, once in a while he'd furrow his brow when something caused him concern, but most of the time he just smiled a very benign smile.

I had arrived at the Twin Cities airport on a Sunday night in the middle of a blizzard, lucky that the flight was not diverted to Chicago or Milwaukee. I took a shuttle to downtown Minneapolis where I had a reservation at a hotel that turned out to be one step up from a flophouse. From my room on one of the upper floors, I looked out the window at the driving snow that was blanketing the city and wondered what in the hell I was doing there.

Actually, it was Part 2 of a four-part plan that went something like this: (1) marry my high school sweetheart; (2) finish the Gale Institute training; (3) land that high-paying job with an airline, preferably somewhere in Northern California; and (4) live happily ever after. Part 1 was completed and my bride of just two short months was waiting for me back in Vallejo. Looking out the window of my room, I don't think I've ever been so lonely. And that was day one!

The next morning, I found my way to the school, and from there to Mrs. Olsen's house, and once I met Jerry, things started to look up. It was hard not to smile when he was around.

So, the three of us—Danny, Jerry and I—went to work on Orville, trying to convince him that we should find our way to the St. Paul Auditorium to see Johnny Cash. Jerry liked Johnny's music, so it was easy to get him onboard. I pitched in because an adventure in the wilds of St. Paul was preferable to sitting around the house feeling homesick. As it turned out, Orville was a pushover. He agreed to come along and provide the transportation in his four-door Chevy Corvair.

Mrs. Olsen gave us directions and we lit out for the St. Paul Auditorium with plenty of time to spare. It was bitter cold that Friday night, with snow piled in three-foot high drifts along the streets. But the snow ploughs had done their job and the pavement was clear and dry. The directions were good and true and we found the auditorium with no trouble. It was a very large brick structure, built to house a variety of events, from concerts and plays, to basketball and hockey, to the Ice Capades and the occasional tractor pull. On this particular night, it was set up as a dance hall, with tables and chairs arranged all around the outer edge of the dance floor and a bandstand set up on one side.

As we came in, many couples were on the floor, dancing to recorded music. I would guess that the crowd was no more than two hundred and fifty people. We found a spot close to the bandstand and waited for Johnny's show to begin. Finally, the announcer came to the microphone, made a few public service announcements, and then said, "And now... please welcome... Johnny Cash and the Tennessee Three!"

Johnny and his band mates bounded onto the stage and launched into their first number. I was shocked to see how thin and gaunt he looked. I attributed it to the rigors of life on the road. Later, of course, we'd learn that Johnny was in the middle of a very dark period in his life, when he was addicted to prescription drugs—uppers and downers— and to alcohol. He looked very nervous and jumpy, and he seemed unhappy with the sound system. Still, the band plunged on and I had the sense that they were giving us the best they had to give in spite of the cavernous room, the iffy sound system, and the small crowd.

The set rolled on, and though I don't remember all the numbers they played, I do remember "I Guess Things Happen That Way," which is a terrific song. Throughout the set, Johnny would periodically cup his right ear with his hand. It seemed an odd gesture and I wondered if there was a purpose, or if it was just an affectation. At one point, he paused to introduce the band. The only name I caught was that of the drummer, "Fluke" Holland. Johnny said he was the drummer on the legendary recording of "Blue Suede Shoes." That drew a respectful round of applause from the crowd. After about forty-five minutes, Johnny said that they were taking a break and would be back soon for the second set.

During the break, Jerry and Orville headed off in search of a cold drink. Danny and I started to join them when suddenly, Danny yelped, "Hey, there's Luther Perkins!" Standing off to the side of the bandstand, smoking a cigarette, was the thin, laid-back guy I recognized as the electric guitar player. Danny grabbed my arm and we hurried over to say hello.

Danny could barely contain himself, gushing to Luther that he was a great fan of their music and generally acting the way most of us would when standing face to face with one of our heroes. Luther was very friendly and accommodating, as though he welcomed this impromptu meeting. I asked him why Johnny kept cupping his right ear. He said that in a huge space like this one, the sound tends to get lost. Cupping his ear allowed him to hear his voice and judge how he was coming across.

We chatted a little longer and then Luther said, "Where are you guys from?"

Danny jumped right in. "My name is Danny and I'm from Waterloo, Iowa. And Charlie here is from a place nobody ever heard of—Vallejo, California."

"Vallejo?" Luther said. "Oh, we've played there many times, at the Dream Bowl out on Highway 29."

I looked at Danny and saw his jaw drop about three inches and I couldn't help but laugh out loud. Luther finished his cigarette, shook our hands and thanked us for coming out, and then headed off to regroup for the second set. I think Danny was still in shock and I managed to slip in a few zingers about *a place nobody ever heard of.* It was good fun.

We stayed through the second set, watching the Tennessee Three and their star giving it their level best. The song I remember from that set was "The Rebel… Johnny Yuma." After Johnny said thank you and goodnight, we headed back out into the cold for the long drive back to Mrs. Olsen's.

On the way home, Danny held forth on all things Johnny Cash. How Luther Perkins is credited with creating their distinctive "boom chicka boom" sound. How Luther and Marshall Grant, the bass player, were originally the Tennessee Two. Then W.S. "Fluke" Holland joined the band and they became the Tennessee Three. And the recording of "Blue Suede Shoes" that Fluke played on was the Carl Perkins original, before Elvis covered it. And Carl Perkins, who wrote "Blue Suede Shoes," was no relation to Luther, though some people think they are brothers. And on and on…

We took Danny's word for all of this, and at the end of the day, I knew more about country music than I really wanted to know. Of course, there were many things that were unknowable on that cold night in late March, a night when the Minnesota winter held on tight and refused to give way to spring. I could not know, for instance, that at the end of the Gale program, I would accept a job with Northwest Airlines and ask my bride to pack everything we owned and move to Minnesota. I couldn't know that we would live there for three years and our two beautiful daughters would be born there, or that we would meet wonderful people who would become our dearest friends. And I couldn't know then that happily ever after was not in the cards for us. All of that was in the future.

At that moment, riding home through the bleak streets of the Twin Cities, I was happy and even exhilarated. I felt that somehow I had scored a victory for my hometown. Thanks to a major assist from Luther Perkins, it was Vallejo 1, Waterloo 0.

Sociology 1A

A Memoir of the Sixties

Cleaning out a closet one day, you opened a box and there on the top of the stack of papers was your transcript from Merritt College in Oakland. You hadn't seen it in forty years. You scanned the list of classes you completed and, lo and behold, there it was: Sociology 1A. And you could not help but smile at the memory of those hectic days long ago.

You remember the first night of class—was it fall semester '68?— you were late as usual. You parked on Grove Street, a couple of blocks from the campus and took off on a flat-out sprint, just as you had so many nights before. You ran by the barbeque joint where an old black man was standing outside, taking a smoke break, and he called to you *Hey, Lickidysplit, you late for class again? Ha ha ha!* Without breaking stride, you shouted back *You got that right. See ya later.* And he said *Not if I see you first! Ha ha ha!* The laughter followed you down the street and you promised yourself that someday you'd stop there for some barbeque because it smelled like heaven.

You bounded up the steps of the main building, up the staircase to the second floor and into the classroom. You grabbed a desk at the back of the class. The instructor was reading aloud from a text of some sort and twenty-some-odd students were hanging on every word. *Is he reading from the textbook?* you asked the guy sitting next to you. *No, it's a poem. I think he said it's by Robinson Jeffers.* You checked out the instructor. He was wearing a plaid wool shirt, jeans, motorcycle boots. Perched on his nose was a pair of round granny glasses. His hair was long and shaggy. He looked like John Lennon gone to seed. He finished with a line that said something about *life crawling out of the primordial ooze onto dry land.* He closed the book with a thump, then fake-stumbled off of the desk where he'd been sitting and said *Now that is heavy!* The class gave him a round of applause.

You sat there wondering what the hell this had to do with sociology. The instructor launched into a discussion of the class syllabus and the text that was required. He said to buy it used; don't waste money on the new edition. And in less than an hour, it was class dismissed. Maybe it was because you were tired, or stressed out with too many things to do, but you started to think about dropping this class. You were trying to take two classes that semester but it was too much. You needed to drop a class and this one, with the John Lennon wannabe, was the prime candidate.

You started to go forward to speak to the instructor but he was surrounded by eager students, most of them girls who thought he was way cute, and so you decided to give it one more week. You would see how the next class went and then you would decide. At least he was letting you out early and you could go home and read bedtime stories to your girls, maybe catch a catnap before heading to work at midnight. In a minute, you were down the stairs and back out on Grove Street.

––––

Ambition came to you late in life. At first you thought that all you needed was a job, any job, to put food on the table and a roof over your head. And so you got married and got that job and two beautiful daughters came along. And then you realized that food on the table and a roof over your head were not enough. You were working for bosses who were no smarter than you, but they had something you didn't: a degree; that magical piece of paper that says you are an educated person. No, just a job was not enough. Not nearly enough. Plus, you wanted the world for your kids. So you hatched a plan. Go back to school, finish your second year of college, do it on the cheap at a community college, make sure your classes were transferrable. You were working and living in the East Bay so Merritt College in Oakland would do just fine. Then you would transfer to Sacramento State, move the family to Fair Oaks, take over a house there that your brother had offered to you. Your wife would work, you would work part-time, your mom would watch the kids. And in three years or so, with any luck, you'd be finished. You would be that educated person. There would be no stopping you. What a plan!

And so there you were, working as a computer operator at Lawrence Radiation Lab—UC Berkeley; working the graveyard shift because it paid a fifteen percent differential; working part-time for Grodins Men's

Wear selling Florsheims in their shoe department; your wife earning extra money providing daycare for a working mom.

You didn't know it then, but what you needed was a Plan B.

———

Berkeley, California. The People's Republic of Berkeley. Berserkeley. Scarborough Faire. Call it what you want, in the mid- to late-sixties it was an interesting place to be. You were hired at LRL Berkeley in the spring of 1965, just in time for the denouement of Mario Savio and the Free Speech Movement. He stood in Sproul Plaza and declared victory over the UC Administration and then said *Hey, don't leave yet. We've still got a war to stop.* And so the FSM morphed into the anti-Vietnam War movement and things went from interesting to radical.

There were nights driving to work when you got off the freeway at University Avenue and were greeted by a police barricade, an officer shining his flashlight in your face asking *What's your business here?* You knew then that another demonstration had gone out of control. You remember the night you came to work and the guys on the evening shift described the helicopter that hovered over Sproul Plaza and dropped teargas to disburse the demonstrators. Then there was the night that some radicals (terrorists?) bombed a tower on the power line feeding the Lab and you sat in the dark until dawn, the only light in the building coming from battery powered lanterns mounted on the walls, half of them inoperative due to neglect.

And down in Oakland, not far from the Merritt campus, was the headquarters of the Black Panther Party, where a couple of off-duty Oakland cops drove by and shot out the windows. The Black Panthers scared the hell out of you—then. It was only later that you and most of your friends read *Soul on Ice* and you all wore "Free Huey" buttons and Tom Wolfe coined the phrase *radical chic.* Thankfully, you were gone by the time the Symbionese Liberation Army showed up and kidnapped Patty Hearst.

The vast majority of students on campus wore the non-conformist uniform: faded jeans, boots or sandals, battered old shirts or sweaters (preferably black), long shaggy hair, and lots of facial hair. And those were the girls! (Just kidding.) But you weren't part of that. You had other

45

priorities. You had a family to support and you had The Plan, and by God you were sticking to it.

May you live in interesting times. Is that a blessing or a curse?

———

Sundays were beautiful. It was your day off. No work at LRL, no classes to attend, no shoes to sell—except during the Christmas season. Sundays were family days. You'd take the bicycles from the patio, buckle the kids into the seats mounted on the back and hit the streets of Alameda. You lived at the north end of the island, close to the Naval Air Station, but the city had a fine system of bike lanes and bike-friendly neighborhoods to ride in. Alameda was a small town set down in the middle of a teaming metropolis. Your favorite thing to do was to ride out past the Southshore Shopping Center to the beach that faced San Francisco Bay. The kids could play in the sand for hours while you kicked back with a book, or enjoyed an adult conversation with your wife. Off to the northwest you had a great view of the Bay Bridge and the skyline of downtown San Francisco, a city that you'd always loved. And then you'd load the kids back onto the bikes and head for home, through the beautiful neighborhoods, wondering how much those homes were worth and if you could ever afford one.

Maybe it was something you could add to The Plan.

———

The second class session of Sociology 1A wasn't much better than the first. The instructor held forth, displaying his snappy sense of humor, soaking up all the laughter, and generally enjoying the spotlight the classroom afforded him. Again you wondered what the hell this had to do with sociology and you were glad you hadn't purchased the text. You made it through to the break without walking out. You approached Mr. Lennon and told him you had to drop the class and he began trying to talk you out of it. *Hey, stick it out. It's not going to be so bad. No papers to write. Whataya say?* You told him you couldn't do it and would he please just turn in a drop for you and finally, reluctantly, he agreed. He shook your hand and wished you well as you headed for the door.

That's that you said to yourself. Yeah, right.

Working at LRL was a good gig. The computer center, situated in the Admin building way up on the hill behind the Berkeley campus, supported the Physics Department and graduate students who were assigned to one of several groups. The physics groups were headed by some of the best known scientists in the field of high-energy particle physics, men like Dr. Luis Alvarez. By the mid-sixties, there were six or seven Nobel laureates associated with the Lab.

The mission of the computer center was to process all the data collected in experiments conducted utilizing LRL's Cyclotron (invented by Dr. Ernest Lawrence), a particle accelerator that sent beams of protons crashing into target mater and recorded the results when atoms split and sub-atomic particles went spinning off through a bubble chamber.

You also worked with the grad students as they learned to use the large-scale computer systems. They studied FORTRAN and other languages and wrote programs to perform dubious functions, all in the name of higher learning. You got a kick out of seeing the new students arrive each fall, neatly shaven and trimmed, wearing their sport coats and ties, their wingtip oxfords shined to a high gloss. You'd take bets on how long it would take them to don the Berkeley uniform: jeans, sandals, shaggy hair, beards. It didn't take long—about three weeks, max. You wondered what their families thought when they went home for the holidays.

But it was a good gig. You worked with lots of great guys and the occasional great gal. (Let's face it: sexism was still rampant in the job market.) There was Hugh, a hard worker and a true friend, an older version of you: in his early forties, married with two daughters, working two jobs to make ends meet. There was Roger B, a smart-mouthed, cocky kid, always fun, always funny. There was Brian, who spent most of his free time tracking down his pot connection; needless to say, a very mellow guy. There was Roger G, who had moved on from grass to LSD and was evangelical on the benefits of chemical mind-expansion.

On the graveyard shift, midnight to eight, things got very quiet around 3:00 a.m. You'd fire up the long jobs that processed all that experimental data and then do your best to stay awake. One good thing to do was to step out onto the balcony that looked out across the bay to the Golden Gate Bridge. God, what a view! It was ever-changing and you never tired of it. The best, the one you'll never forget, was the full moon hanging over the north tower of the bridge, a river of yellow light streaming across the bay to the Berkeley shore. San Francisco was off to the left, with the Top of the Mark and the lighted elevator shaft that reached the Crown Room at the Fairmont perched high up on Nob Hill. Standing there, looking out across the bay, you were absolutely certain that anything was possible.

Wasn't that the way a guy in his mid-twenties was supposed to feel?

———

Sleep was hard to come by at home. It seemed you were always in transition, from sleeping during the day, to sleeping at night on your days off, and then back to the night shift routine. Somehow in the transitions, you lost a day and half of sleep, or so it seemed.

Your wife did the best she could to keep the kids quiet and occupied. This included your two vivacious daughters and the little boy she took care of, a nervous little bird named Donnie. He was nearly two and still in diapers and he cried a lot. You could hold him and comfort him and calm his crying, but smiles were hard to come by, and laughter just wasn't part of Donnie's personality. But the thing that made Donnie unique, that set him apart from all of his peers, was the fact that when he pooped his pants the smell was unbearable. It was so bad it could trigger your gag reflex. You had to tie a bandanna around your face like a cowboy in order to change his diaper, and even that didn't help much. You found yourself asking *What the hell is your mother feeding you?*

Your shift at LRL ended at 8:00 a.m. There was a great donut shop (it reminded you of Scotty's in Vallejo) on the north edge of the campus, right on your way home, and now and then you'd stop and pick up a mixed dozen for the family. Generally, you were home in bed asleep by 9:00 a.m. and wide-awake around 3:00 in the afternoon. Then it was time to get up and help take care of the kids.

You'd pray that Donnie would hold his fire until after his mom picked him up.

———

Several evenings each week and most Saturdays, you drove up Highway 24, through the Caledecott Tunnel and on to Walnut Creek, to sell shoes at Grodins. Fred was the department manager, a great guy who became a friend for life. Freddie had a line of malarkey that was perfect for talking a customer out of his old shoes and into a new pair of Florsheims. Years earlier, when he first applied for a job at Grodins, the store manager asked him *What do you know about men's clothes?* Freddie said *Well, I've been wearing 'em since I was fifteen.* The manager cracked up laughing and hired Freddie on the spot. Brash, cocky, funny, and a pretty good golfer, too—that's Fred.

The Bay Area stores were covered by the Retail Clerks Union, so you were paid a flat hourly wage, or six percent commission, whichever was greater. Walnut Creek was a good store and you always made commission. Actually, you made out pretty well for a part-time job.

Occasionally they'd assign you to work at the Grodins in Berkeley, on Telegraph Avenue just south of Sather Gate. That location was dying a slow death because most of the students shopped at the local Army-Navy Surplus store. You'd stand around and watch the colorful scene out on Telegraph Avenue, watching the clock tick slowly toward closing time, wishing you were back in the Walnut Creek action.

Or home in bed asleep.

————

It was a bright January day and you were going through the mail, and there it was: the envelope from Merritt College with the grade report for the fall semester. You opened it and saw that you had earned an A in the class that you completed. And then on the next line you read: *Sociology 1A – Incomplete.* Holy crap! John Lennon didn't turn in a drop; he gave you an incomplete.

After work the next morning, you headed for the Merritt campus to take up the issue with the front office. The lady at the counter listened sympathetically and then told you that only the instructor could change the grade report. Unfortunately, Mr. Lennon wasn't teaching a class in the spring semester and wouldn't be on campus. So, she looked up his phone number and gave him a call; the phone was disconnected. You stressed the urgency of the matter, that you had to submit your application to Sac State and you needed this corrected ASAP. She thought about it for a while and then said *I'm not supposed to do this, but here is the last address we have for him.*

You jumped in the car and headed for the address on Bancroft Avenue in Berkeley, which turned out to be an apartment building that had seen better days. You found his apartment and rang the bell and he answered with a hearty *Hi, how ya doin'?* like you were a long lost friend. You explained the importance of changing his grade report from an incomplete to a drop, and he immediately launched another attempt to change your mind. *Tell ya what, I'll give you a book, you'll read it and give me a couple-page report and I'll give you a grade. Whataya say?* You said *Thanks, but no thanks.* You didn't add that his proposal offended your sense of ethical behavior. He finally gave up and promised to phone in the change. Then he grinned and waved and wished you well as you hurried away to your car.

That's that you said to yourself—again. But this time you didn't have much confidence.

———

For the most part, your experience at Merritt College had been positive. You'd completed all your general education requirements, maintained a 3.8-plus GPA, taken all the computer science classes you could squeeze in, and generally enjoyed the experience.

Over the course of several semesters, you'd come to know a couple of guys that you enjoyed hanging out with during class breaks. One was a CHP officer, the other a guard at San Quentin. Both were black and though they were farther along in their careers than you, it was amazing how closely their lives paralleled yours. They were concerned for their families, looking to find homes in clean, safe neighborhoods, looking for good schools for their kids. They were just like you and you looked forward to chatting with them every week.

When Martin Luther King was assassinated, suddenly it seemed like a wall had sprung up between you. You felt a decided coolness, as though you weren't welcome in their circle anymore. Even though it was understandable, it hurt, and you never really got over it. Maybe you tried too hard, or said the wrong things? Maybe they just needed to process this devastating loss in their own way? With time, you could have fixed it, and perhaps they'd be your friends to this day; but your time there was running out. It remains one of the few bad memories associated with Merritt College.

Another bad one was the night that the Black Panthers came on campus and locked the Faculty Senate in a meeting room, refusing to let them go until they agreed to the hiring of more black instructors and the development of a black studies curriculum. There was a rumor that Angela Davis was with them but you could never confirm it.

You cut class that night and went home. All you wanted to do was hug your kids.

————

As the spring of '69 progressed, so did The Plan. You moved your family from Alameda to the house in Fair Oaks, your wife went to work for Allstate Insurance, and your mom lived with them during the week to take care of the kids. You continued to work at LRL, living during the week at your mom's home in Vallejo and commuting to Berkeley. Your application to Sac State was in the mail, along with a copy of your transcript. According to plan, you would start the fall semester in Sacramento and work part-time at the Grodins located in Country Club Center.

One morning, for some unknown reason, you decided to call the Merritt College office and check on that grade report, just in case. The woman who answered the phone made sure you were authentic and then went to pull your records. *Sociology 1A? Ah yes, you got an A.* After you picked up your jaw, you thanked her and hung up the phone.

So, John Lennon had changed the incomplete to an A. You had to think about that for a minute. Should you call back and go through the nosebleed of trying—yet again—to get the record corrected? Or not?

You thought about your life. Did it not range from the pristine suburbs of Alameda to the ghetto campus in Oakland, from the radicalized scene at UC Berkeley to the upscale shopping malls of Walnut Creek? In your daily travels, didn't you move in and out of various layers of society, through institutions both revered and reviled? Did you not rub shoulders with stoners, barbeque purveyors, future scientists, and Black Panthers? Isn't sociology the study of society, its systems and institutions, and wasn't your life a field study in progress? If anybody deserved an A in sociology, most certainly it was you.

Damn the ethics! Full speed ahead!

———

It wasn't long after that when The Plan began to fall apart. The *coup de grace* came in the form of a polite letter from Sacramento State College, advising that they could not accept you for the fall term due to an enrollment glut. The letter suggested that you apply at Humboldt State in Arcata, way up north, where the application volume was less impacted. Unfortunately, you now lived in Fair Oaks. Arcata would be a hell of a commute. And so you found a job in the Sacramento area and settled in to work and care for your family, your college dreams deferred for the time being.

That was a long time ago. At three score and ten, it's good that you remember all the people and places, the sights and sounds and smells, and especially what it was like to be so young and alive and lucky, to run down Grove Street with an old man's laughter at your back, sprinting toward a future that would fill your heart, then break it, then fill it again. And all of those memories triggered by a simple line on a transcript:

Class: Sociology 1A / Semester Units: 3 / Grade: A

Sam

Memories of a good dog...

Early in 1977, my wife Barbara and I moved into our brand new home in Citrus Heights, California. It was a two-story, four-bedroom house with a good sized lot and we'd watched it being built from the foundation up. It may seem odd, but the first acquisition we made for our new home was a puppy.

It was the era in Sacramento of the East Area Rapist, a man suspected of upwards of a dozen sexual assaults, all of them in the eastern suburbs of the city. I occasionally had to work nights and travel for business, and we decided that we'd feel safer with a dog in the house, preferably one with big teeth.

Barbara watched the ads in the local paper and saw one for German Shepherd puppies ready for adoption. She drove to the address, checked out the litter, and brought home a beautiful little female with black and tan markings. We consulted with my daughters, Kim and Cheryl, and decided that a right and proper name for this new member of the family would be Samantha. And so, Samantha it was, which we  immediately shortened to just plain Sam. (Of course we couldn't know that thirty-five years later, we'd have a beautiful granddaughter named Samantha.)

I'd grown up with a pet dog, a terrier mutt named George, but this was a first for Barbara. She and Sam formed an immediate bond. Sam wasn't pure bred—I suspect there was some Husky in her bloodlines—but she was a smart little puppy with a sweet and loving nature.

One of the first things Sam learned was to fetch the newspaper for me. I'd open the front door and she'd run out on the walk and bring in the paper. What a good dog! But it was too good to last. One morning, she picked up the paper, turned and looked at me, and then took off running down the walk and across the street. I was in close pursuit, yelling at her to stop, and she made it only as far as the neighbor's yard before she plopped down and waited for me to reach her. Unfortunately, my neighbor had recently planted his lawn and it was just beginning to sprout. Sam wouldn't budge, so I had to walk out onto the new lawn, leaving giant footprints, to retrieve her. I think Sam came to associate the incident with the words "bad dog," because she never again retrieved the paper.

Sam was a healthy puppy. There were only a few occasions when we had to take her to the vet. She was spayed at the appropriate time and came through just fine. She picked up a bad case of kennel cough once when we boarded her for a weekend. But the illness we'll never forget was the vaginal infection.

We could tell that she wasn't herself, so we took her to the vet. He diagnosed the infection, prescribed some pills, and also gave us a tube of salve. We were supposed to insert the extended nozzle and squeeze the tube to apply the medication. Sam was nearly full-grown at the time and she was having none of this. Can you picture trying to pin down a seventy pound German Shepherd to administer this treatment? After what seemed like an hour (it was probably fifteen minutes), in a full sweat and with a cloud of dog hair around us, we finally gave up. The infection went away without the salve.

Sam was very intuitive and quick to pick up on our clues. We planned a camping trip to Bodega Bay one weekend and as I backed our Pinto station wagon into the driveway and started to load the gear, Sam jumped into the back of the car and refused to get out. There was no way we were leaving home without her. It was an interesting trip. Every noise outside the tent at night—be it a raccoon, a bird, or a lizard— would set Sam off barking. We didn't get much sleep that weekend.

As she matured, her watchdog instincts really began to develop. I would say, "Sam, what's that?" and she would take off barking at every door and window, using her best big-dog voice.

One weekend, my mom came to stay with us. In the middle of the night, Sam suddenly started barking like crazy. I sat up in bed and saw someone standing in the hall just outside our bedroom door. I jumped up, grabbed a baseball bat I kept under the bed, and in a very shaky voice said, "Who are you and what are you doing here?" The figure replied, "Charlie, I just have to go to the bathroom." It was my mom. After things calmed down, I said a little prayer of thanks that it wasn't a gun I had stashed under the bed.

In the fall of 1978, we learned that Barbara was pregnant—with twins! We had also realized in the time Sam had been with us that we were allergic to her fur. Now with two little babies on the way, we decided some changes had to be made. I would build a dog run for Sam in the backyard and we would convert her to being an outside dog. The dog run turned out quite nice—large, partially covered, paved, with a shepherd-size dog house. Only one problem: Sam hated it. She just didn't understand why she couldn't be in the house with her people.

One of our neighbors had a beautiful tan Boxer named Hosang who was about Sam's age. Hosang would come over to play and he and Sam would romp and tumble and race around the backyard until they were both exhausted. But as soon as she had to go back into that dog run, she was miserable. She spent most of her time biting the dog wire, trying to chew her way out.

Our twins, Matt and Rachel, were born in May of 1979. When they were nearing their first birthday, we learned that Barb was pregnant again. Gabe would be born when the twins were eighteen months old. It would be like having triplets. All of our energy and attention would be going into caring for three little ones. We knew that we were not giving Sam the care and attention she deserved. We started to talk about trying to find a good home for her.

Then fate intervened.

I was working for Roseville Telephone at the time and the company newsletter hit my desk containing a notice from an employee who was looking for a good dog. Her name is lost to memory, so let's call her Mrs. Parker. I called her and told her I thought I had just the dog she was looking for. We chatted for a while and she told me that she and her husband had a five-acre parcel of land, what is called "horse property" in our area, and that they had two other dogs. The dogs had free run of the property. From our conversation, I could tell she was a true dog lover.

Then she asked her big question: "Is she a barking dog?" I thought, *Uh oh, this could be a deal breaker.* Should I tell a white lie and say Sam was a nice quiet little lady, or should I tell the truth? I took a deep breath and told her all about Sam's watchdog instincts and that, yes, she was a barking dog. Mrs. Parker said, "That's exactly what we're looking for."

We made a date for the Parkers to come over on Sunday and meet Sam. I told them we were having friends over for a barbeque, but to just come around to the gate on the side of the house and I'd let them in. It was understood that if they liked our Sam, they would take her home.

Sunday arrived and we were relaxing on the patio in back of the house when I heard a car pull up out in front. I heard doors slam and I figured it was the Parkers come to see Sam. I said, "Sam, what's that?" and she charged for the gate barking furiously. I took her by the collar and calmed her down, then let the Parkers in. I could see them nodding their heads and smiling at each other. They were sold.

We visited for a while and then they were ready to leave. Barbara hadn't realized that they were taking Sam with them, thinking they would talk it over and call us later. Now she had about five minutes to say goodbye. She sat down on the patio and took Sam in her arms, tears streaming down her face. And then the Parkers clipped a leash to Sam's collar and led her away.

About a month later, I was out at our Citrus Heights central office facility for a meeting. I parked in back of the building near the loading dock and walked over to the fence that bordered the property. It turns out the Parker's five acres were adjacent to the Company's land. I looked out across the field and there were three dogs playing along the fence on the west side. One of them was Sam. I gave a shrill whistle and yelled "Sam!" She stopped dead still and turned to look at me. Just then, her companions took off running at full speed down the fence line. Sam stood for a few seconds and then turned and sprinted after them.

It had been a long time since I'd seen her so happy. For love of Sam, we'd done the right thing.

We Hold These Truths

Author's note: This story was originally posted as fiction. It is a true story with the names changed, so it is included here among the non-fiction pieces. In case you are wondering, Carl is yours truly. I'm sorry to admit it, but it's true.

Carl sipped his coffee and unfolded the morning newspaper. It was November 5, 2008, and there on the front page was a picture of the president-elect and his beaming family. He thought about the speech from Grant Park the night before, with the repeated refrain "Yes, we can," and the silent echoes of "I have a dream …"

And then it all came rushing back, a full-blown flashback to October, 1962. He could remember standing in the kitchen of the old apartment in Minneapolis, fumbling around in the drawer to find the business card, dialing the number and waiting nervously as the phone began to ring. And of course, he remembered the conversation verbatim…

"Hello."

"Hi, Sean. It's Carl."

"Hi, kid. What's up?"

"I showed the apartment today."

"Already? The ad just started today. You probably just put the sign out. Good work! Did you rent it?"

"Uh … not exactly."

"Whataya mean?"

"Well, two guys showed up at the door bright and early, both of 'em wearing full dress Air Force uniforms. One was a Captain Jordan and the other said he was his commanding officer, but I didn't get his rank. They were looking for an apartment for Jordan."

"Yeah, so?"

"Well, Captain Jordan is colored."

"Oh crap. So what did you do?

"I showed them the apartment."

57

"You did what? Why did you do that, Carl?"

"We ran the ad, Sean. We've got a sign out front that says 'apartment for rent.' What was I supposed to do?"

"So what happened?"

"So, Jordan looked it over. Meantime the old man tells me that Jordan is a bomber pilot. They don't have housing for him and he needs a place close to the airport and the Air National Guard base, for him and his family."

"Family? Oh great."

"Yeah, wife and two little boys."

"So what happened?"

"Well, Jordan liked it and wanted to take it. So I had him fill out the application."

"You did what?!"

"Keep your shirt on. I told him there were two other applications that we're checking out and it's first come, first served. If one of the apps checks out, the apartment is rented."

"Okay, okay ... good thinking. What did they say?"

"The old man gave me the fish eye, but they said thanks and left."

"Okay, here's what you do: wait until about noon, then call and say it's rented. Case closed."

"What about the sign? What if they drive by and see it's still there?"

"Good point. Okay, bring in the sign. We still got the ad running. I'll explain it to the company."

"I don't know, Sean. It doesn't feel right. The whole thing feels wrong."

"What? Why? You know the company's policy. We're not renting to coloreds in that building. Not in that neighborhood. If we did, then what? What about the next apartment, and the one after that? Before you know it, it would be the entire building. They have their own part of town, Carl. Why aren't they looking there, with their own people, for God's sake?"

"I know, but the guy is a B-47 pilot, Sean. You know what's going on. Kennedy has the naval blockade going. Russian ships are heading for Cuba. Who knows what that crazy-ass Khrushchev is going to do next? We could be at war in a couple of days. Besides, Jordan seemed like a nice guy. It doesn't feel right, Sean."

"Look, Carl, I don't make the rules. I work for the company and you report to me. I'm gonna keep my job, and I'm sure you want to keep that nice manager's apartment with the discounted rent. So call him back and tell him it's rented. Got it?

"Yeah, Sean. I 'got it'."

"Don't crack wise with me, kid. Just do what I told you. Or I'll get somebody who will."

With that, the line went dead.

Later that day, Carl remembered standing next to the wall-mounted phone in the kitchen, working up the courage to make the call, rehearsing what he would say. *I'm sorry, but the apartment has been rented. Thanks for your application and good luck ... good luck with that possible war thing ... hope you don't have to fly off to Havana...or Moscow.* He dialed the first six digits of the number Jordan had left, and then waited, his finger poised to dial the seventh.

"Hell with it," he said out loud, banging the phone back into the cradle.

He never made the call. Like many other things, he just didn't have the guts for it. The company continued to prosper, with its little red lines drawn on the map. Sean kept his job, enforcing those red lines, and Captain Jordan presumably kept his, defending the American way.

Carl looked at the front page again and smiled. He'd have to save this edition, maybe round up a few more copies for his kids and grandkids. October of 1962 was a long time ago—and so very far away.

Rush to Limbaughland

December 2, 2008

I turned on the radio the other day and there was a certain oversized talk show host in full-throated attack mode over something the president-elect said in a press conference. It occurred to me that the election of Barack Obama was the best thing that could have happened to The Large One, a virtual guarantee of four years of fresh material. That is...if he sticks around. What do I mean by that? Well, I heard a rumor. It goes like this:

> Starting in January, there will be a mass relocation of disgruntled dittoheads and neo-cons, heading for Alaska, where they will all join the Alaska Independence Party. Alaska will then secede from the union and become an independent nation-state known as Limbaughland. But wait, there is more:

- Sarah Palin will run unopposed for president with Joe the Plumber as her running mate.
- Tom DeLay, Larry Craig, Ted Stevens, and John Doolittle will all be nominated and confirmed to the Supreme Court.
- Arnold Schwarzenegger will resign as governor of California and join the Palin administration as Budget Director.
- Jack Abramoff will be named Secretary of Commerce and immediately announce groundbreaking for a new Neiman-Marcus store in Wasilla.
- President Palin will contact U.S. President Obama and suggest a summit meeting—with no preconditions.

The rumor doesn't include anything about a national anthem for Limbaughland, but there are reports of a marching song with a familiar theme:

> "Who's the leader of the state that's great for you and me? /
> H-O-C-K-E-Y M-O-M-M-Y…"

Like I said, it's a rumor. Maybe you heard it too?

Bike Trail Boy

Let's hear it for the American River Bike Trail! It is a wonderful resource, all thirty-two miles of it, from Folsom Lake to Discovery Park and the Sacramento River. We live near the midway point at mile thirteen, and it seems almost criminal to live so close and not take advantage. That's what brought me to Carmichael Cycle one Sunday last summer.

I'd browsed around Carmichael Cycle (cute name, eh?) before, but this time I was a serious shopper. I was determined to buy a bike. The only question was, what kind? As it turns out, there are many choices. There are mountain bikes, and racing bikes, and street bikes, and regular old fat tire bikes that have been re-christened "beach cruisers," even though we don't have a beach to cruise.

The young man at the shop showed me some classic skinny-tire racing bikes with equally skinny seats, the bicycle equivalent of thong underwear. He said they were for "aggressive" riders. I can see why a seat like that would make you aggressive. These bikes had narrow handlebars that curled like rams horns and looked like you had to stay in a permanent tuck position to ride one. I told him I don't tuck much anymore.

We finally found a row of bikes with upright handlebars and wider, flatter seats. He told me they were "comfort bikes." Now that's more like it! After a quick test ride, I became the proud owner of a comfort bike. I also bought a stand that turns the bike into a stationary trainer so that I can work out indoors during bad weather. I have to admit, I haven't put many miles on that bike stand. If anyone out there is looking for a bike stand/trainer with very low miles, have I got a deal for you!

And so I hit the trail, riding upstream for five or six miles, or downstream about an equal distance. It is a great workout and the scenery is beautiful, and you really come to appreciate the change of seasons. The difference between July and December is quite striking.

My comfort bike has a feature that has caused me some concern. There is a bell attached to the handlebars. It has a little spring-loaded lever that you flick with your thumb to make it ring. I assumed it was to alert other bike trail users when you are approaching, and that all bikes would be equipped with one. When son Gabe saw it, he just laughed. Son Matt was a little more respectful, but I could tell he was amused.

I learned straight away the difference between Aggressive and Comfort bikers. I can be clipping along at what I think is a pretty good pace and suddenly I'll hear, "On your left," followed by a whooshing sound as the rider flies past. That is an Aggressive. Sometimes they ride in teams. You hear, "On your left—four!" followed closely by whoosh-whoosh-whoosh-whoosh.

You can tell the Aggressives by their bike shorts that look painted on, their little magic shoes that clip on to the peddles, their colorful biking shirts or windbreakers, and a myriad of other gear—rear-view mirrors, water bottles, saddlebags, and so forth—but no bells on the handlebars.

We Comfort types, on the other hand, are usually in T-shirts and shorts during the warm months, or old sweatshirts and jogging suits when the weather turns. On our feet you will find running shoes that became walking shoes on their way to becoming biking shoes. Many of us don't bother to wear a helmet. What is the worst that can happen at Comfort speed?

My favorite route is downstream on the trail to Howe Avenue, then over to University Avenue, then on to American River Drive and back home. It's about ten miles and it's enough for me.

One Sunday I was clipping along toward Howe Avenue when I saw a unusual rider up ahead. As I got closer, I could see that it was a woman with curly gray hair popping out of her helmet riding a three-wheeler. "On your left," I called out as I prepared to pass. I glanced to my right as I went by with a semi-whoosh and the lady smiled at me and rang the prominent bell attached to her handlebars. I'm guessing that she was in her mid-seventies.

I intend to ride the bike trail every chance I get, maybe adding a little distance each trip. I know what you're thinking, but I'm definitely not ready for a three-wheeler. And one of these days I'm going to find my crescent wrench and take that damn bell off my bike.

Johnny B

December 11, 2008

Early last month, I was riding my bike on the home leg of a ten mile trek and I happened past the baseball field at Rio Americano High School. There were two lonely figures out on the diamond, one throwing pitches from behind an L-screen in front of the mound, and the other a left-handed hitter taking swings at the offerings. The ball seemed to jump off the bat and a couple of them flew deep into the parking lot beyond the right field fence. Then it dawned on me: *I think I know who that is!*

I pulled over and parked by the backstop and watched the hitter sending line drives deep into the outfield. The pitcher exhausted his ball bag and the two of them started to jog after the balls to retrieve them for another round. As the hitter approached the backstop, I called out to him.

"Hi, John. It's Chuck Spooner … Matt and Gabe's dad."

"Oh … Hi, Mr. Spooner. How are you?"

John Bowker, outfielder/first baseman for the San Francisco Giants, came out from behind the backstop and walked toward me, his hand outstretched, sweat dripping from his forehead even though it was a cool evening. As I shook his hand, it was clear that he is no longer the skinny kid I used to see down at the Arden Little League fields. The Giants' media guide lists him at six feet two inches, two hundred pounds, and it looks to be all muscle. Kids do grow up.

We chatted for a while and he told me that he has bumped into Gabe a few times around town, but that he hasn't seen Matt since his junior varsity season at Rio when Matt was the assistant JV coach. I caught him up on the current status of all the Spooner kids.

I told John how much I enjoyed watching Giants' games last summer when he was called up from Fresno. John arrived swinging a hot bat and became the first player in Giants' history to hit a home run in each of his first two games. Think about that: for a franchise that boasts such names as Mays, McCovey, Cepeda, Jim Ray Hart, Bobby Bonds, and Will Clark, that's really saying something. Of course, John's bat cooled off as bats are inclined to do, and it was back to Fresno for a while. We talked a while longer and then I let him get back to work. I could tell he wanted to get in some more swings before the sun went down.

The following Friday, I was passing Rio again and saw John and his friend leaving the diamond after another workout. I waved to him as I passed and he called out, "Hi, Mr. Spooner." I had the feeling that if I peddled by every day, John would be there, working on his game.

February will roll around soon and ballplayers from all over the world will migrate to Florida and Arizona for spring training, that magical time when all thirty major league teams are tied for first place. I think we should keep a good thought and a prayer for John Bowker as he tries to make the team and win a contract for the coming season.

May his eye be keen
May his bat be swift
May the line drives flow like a mighty stream
And may his splash hits rain on McCovey Cove like a summer shower.

Can I get an Amen?

I'm sure of one thing: whether he is in Fresno or San Francisco, John Bowker isn't going to change much. His parents raised a fine young man.

Grapes Revisited

There is a chapter in Steinbeck's *The Grapes of Wrath* where the Joad family pulls into a government-run camp. After weeks on the road, spending the nights in Hoovervilles—under bridges, alongside ditches and streams, anywhere with a water source—they find themselves in an organized camp. There are designated campsites, fresh water faucets, and—wonder of wonders—a building that houses restrooms, showers, and laundry facilities. There is a chain-link fence around the place to keep the residents secure, and a manager who watches the gate and collects a nominal fee. But the camp is essentially run by a committee of the residents. All residents must do their part to keep the place safe and clean.

This abrupt change is a bit of a shock. The Joads have become accustomed to living in the dirt, seeing police raids swoop down and break up whatever Hooverville they found themselves in. This camp polices itself. Break the rules and you are asked to leave.

What's the point, Chuck?

There was a report on television news last night (December 29, 2011), and an article in the newspaper this morning, about the Sacramento Police breaking up a tent city of about one hundred and fifty illegal campers along the American River. These homeless folks were told on Wednesday that if they were not gone by Thursday, their tents will be torn down and their belongings confiscated.

All of this is taking place within a stone's throw of the site where we propose to build a four hundred million dollar sports and entertainment center. City leaders are working hard to find sources of funding—parking revenue, a tax on hotel rooms and rental cars, cash from the Maloof family and the NBA, an investment from the AEG Corporation—to make this dream a reality. This project could be a wonderful boon to the city.

And the construction workers and the illegal campers will be able to keep an eye on one another.

Yes, the city is right to break up the camp. Yes, these campers pose a sanitation and health hazard that can't be tolerated. Yes, many of them are there due to bad choices about drugs and alcohol, not to mention mental illness. Yes, there are a growing number of children among them, because they chose bad parents. And yes, even if you offered warm, dry shelter, many of them would not accept. All this is true.

But I keep coming back to Steinbeck's depiction of the government camp, and I ask myself if there isn't a better way. The simple truth is this: *The Grapes of Wrath* is a classic for good reason. The faces change, the context changes, but we have never finished *trampling out the vintage*.

A Father's Day Message

Author's note: The following is the final message in an e-mail exchange between Harry Diavatis and me. Harry publishes a weekly newsletter titled The Monday Update.

Hi, Harry –

When you asked me to write a few paragraphs about my father and what he meant to me, at first I said *No, sorry, don't have time*. But it has been running around my noggin ever since, so here goes.

My father was the one who taught me to throw and catch a baseball, beginning (according to family legend) when I was three. More than that, he taught me to love the game, something I was later able to share with my kids.

My father was the guy who took me with him on Saturday mornings to cash his paycheck from the shipyard. This included a bus ride to the Skipper's Club, then up Virginia Street to the original Relay, then over to the Towne House on Georgia Street, and finally, back on the bus for the ride home. Saloon hopping with Dad was my favorite thing to do when I was five.

My father shared his love of professional wrestling—yes, wrestling!— and took me to the Farragut Club on Georgia Street to see the likes of Leo Nomellini, the Sharp Brothers, and Antonio Rocca.

My father gave me his work ethic, the drive to work longer and harder than the next guy. It has been a blessing, and at times, a curse. And of course, there is the related lesson: A Good Sailor always cleans up his own mess.

My father gave me his politics and the deeply ingrained belief that a working man has only two things going for him: his union and the Democratic Party. If he knew I voted for Ronald Reagan, he would never forgive me.

As I reached my teens, I found that I was angry with him much of the time. He was a hard man, and neither one of us could bend. And then he was gone, lost to a stroke and a heart attack, and we never had a chance to make amends.

But when I look in the mirror now, there he is. A little taller, a little thinner, and with more hair, but it's my dad nonetheless. We're still working it out, him and me. But things are getting better all the time.

Thanks, Harry. And Happy Father's Day.

A Good, Good Man

Note: My in-laws, Archie & Shirley Vine, came to live with us in August of 2010. Archie was in failing health after suffering a stroke in December of 2008. He passed away on Friday, May 6, 2011. The following are my remarks at his funeral on Monday, May 9.

I want to thank all of you for being here today. This is wonderful tribute to my father-in-law. And I want you to know what an honor it is for me to say "a few words" about Archie Vine. I have so many words I could share that we  would be here for a long time, so I'll give you the condensed version.

I was going to start with the word **Dividends** and tell you how Dad famously said one Thanksgiving, "Mom and I invested all of our lives, and all of you (meaning his children, grandchildren, their spouses, and his great grandchildren) are our Dividends."

I was going to mention **MegaMillions and SuperLotto** because Dad always, always believed he was going to hit the lottery. And when he did, he would provide security for his entire family.

I was going to talk about being Dad's **Newsboy,** getting up early in the morning to read the newspaper and make a fresh pot of coffee, because Archie loved a good cup of coffee first thing in the morning. And then, after breakfast, I'd sit with Dad to discuss the news of the day.

I was going to mention **Jeopardy** and how we'd play along every evening at 6:30. And when the announcer said, "And now, here's the host of Jeopardy, Alex Tribeck!" Dad, in sync with the announcer, would make a fist with his right hand, punch the air and say, "Tribeck!"

I was going to talk about **Laughter** and Dad's exquisite sense of humor, how he loved to joke with you, and be a gentle tease. And of course his famous line on the occasion of their sixtieth wedding anniversary when Rabbi Taff called Archie and Shirley to the pulpit to say a special blessing. The Rabbi asked Dad, "What is the secret to your long and happy marriage?" Dad said: "Always tell your wife those words she wants to hear: 'Yes, Dear.'"

I was going to tell you about Archie and Shirley, the **Superfans,** and how they attended countless baseball, basketball, football and soccer games for grandsons Marc, Matt, and Gabe. And let's not forget dance recitals, musical reviews and plays for granddaughters Lisa and Rachel. They were—literally—always there.

What I want to do is get directly to the really, really important words. And the first one is **Vuluma;** Mere and Sam Vuluma and their son Jon. Mere joined our family about four years ago to be Archie and Shirley's caregiver, and to see Mere care for them is to witness a thousand acts of loving-kindness every day. Mere is truly an amazing human being.

When Archie suffered a stroke in December of 2008, Mere came up to me at one point, put her arms around me and gave me a hug. She told me how sorry she was that this was happening to Archie. And then she said, "I told my Sam, this is a good, good man." Mere, no one could say it better.

After Dad's stroke, Sam joined the team to stay with Dad through the night and be there if he called out for any reason. Then Sam would stay for breakfast, to talk and laugh and share the news of the day. Archie considered Sam to be his best friend.

When Archie and Shirley moved in with us, Sam would stop by the house to visit.

He'd wrap his arms around Archie and put his hand on Dad's heart and say, "Archie, *Baruch atah Adonai, eloheinu melach h'olam* (Blessed art thou, eternal our God, ruler of the universe). I love you, Archie." And you could see Dad's spirits rise.

Here's my point: if someone asks you if there are angels in this world, the answer is: Yes, and they come from Fiji.

And now here's the most important word to remember about Archie, and that is: **Shirley.** Shirley Kramer Vine. She was the absolute love of his life. Married for very near sixty-five years. His first thought every morning, his last thought every night, and every waking moment in between, was for her care and well-being. To see them together was to be inspired, to be moved, to be renewed.

Whenever he could reach her, he wanted to hold her hand. And then, of course, there were those kisses. First thing in the morning, and right before he went to bed at night, we would line up their chairs so that Archie could put his arm around Shirley, and then he would plant a big, wet, passionate kiss on Shirley's lips.

To which Mere would say, "Oy yi yi!" Which is Fijian for Oy Vey! And Shirley would say, "Delicious!"

They were truly a couple for the ages.

I want to close with a couple of very personal notes, first for myself, and then for Barbara.

Archie Vine was more than just a father-in-law. I lost my father when I was sixteen, and over the years, Archie became a father to me. He was there with his wisdom when I needed advice. He was there with a pep talk when I was feeling low. And, he was there to kick me in the butt a few times when I needed it.

When my own father, and my brother, and my mother passed away, there were words left unspoken and I'll always regret it. With Archie and me, there was nothing left unsaid. I loved him and I told him so. In fact, for the last nine months, I got to tell him every day.

He loved me and told me I was a son to him. What an honor to hear those words! He was simply the most loved and respected man I've ever known.

And now, for Barbara: When Archie and Shirley came to live with us, Barbara and Dad developed a ritual that they observed every night. After Archie gave Shirley that big, wet kiss, Mere would take him and get him ready for bed, and when he was safely tucked in, Barbara would go in to say goodnight. They would talk for a while, and then they would have a dialog that went like this:

Barb: "Good night, Daddy"

Archie: "Good night, sweetheart."

Barb: "I love you, God bless you."

Archie: "I love you too. God bless you and Chuck and your children."

Barb: (lightheartedly) "See you in the morning."

And then she'd wait for him to respond in kind. If he didn't respond, she'd say it again... and again... until they were both laughing. And finally, he'd say:

"See you in the morning."

And then she could leave the room and hope to do it all again the next night.

And so, that's it... a few words about Archie Vine. Remember those words: **Dividends, MegaMillions & SuperLotto, Newsboy, Jeopardy, Laughter, Superfans, Mere & Sam Vuluma**, and of course **Shirley**.

When you hear those words in the days ahead I want you to smile, because this good, good man is at peace.

Shirley Vine

Note: My mother-in-law, Shirley Vine, passed away on October 10, 2012, at the age of ninety-one. The following are my remarks at her funeral on October 12.

I think I can break my relationship with my mother-in-law into three phases. Let's simply call them beginning, middle, and end. In the beginning, I think she was a little skeptical—for reasons I won't go into. She wasn't sure I was the right one for her Barbara. But,  eventually I won her over. That led to the long, happy middle phase of our relationship.

We developed a great rapport and a genuine love for each other. Whenever the opportunity presented itself, especially after Shirley and Archie moved from Chicago to Sacramento, Shirley and I could sit and talk for hours. The subject could be anything: politics, current affairs, religion, books, movies, raising children—it didn't matter. The conversation would go on and on. There were a few times when Archie excused himself and went to bed. Mom and I would just keep on talking.

I learned that she was wise and funny, knowledgeable and informed. I think we all remember how she would cut out articles that she read in a newspaper or a magazine and save them in the drawer of the credenza in her dining room. When you came to the house, she'd pull them out and say, "Chuck, I read this article and I thought you'd find it interesting."

Toward the end, probably the last four or five years, that terrible disease began to take her away from us. But even then, there were some good times. As late as the fall of 2010—and Mere can vouch for this—we would sit at the breakfast table and sing what I call sunshine songs. Like the Sesame Street Song: "Sunny day / Chasin' the clouds away…" If it was raining, we'd sing "Every time it rains it rains / Pennies from heaven." Many times, Shirley would join in the singing. And Archie would say, "Can you sing 'Far Far Away'?"

Those are the times to remember. I could tell Shirley Vine stories all day, but I'll try to be brief. There are two things I will always remember about my mother-in-law: Her warmth, and her strength.

Let's start with her warmth and her friendliness. I don't think Shirley Vine ever met a stranger. She relished introducing herself to new people and making new friends. When Shirley and Archie still lived in Chicago and they would fly out to visit two or three times a year, Mom would always come off the plane with one or two business cards in hand. She'd say, "Chuck, I met the most interesting young man on the plane. I think he does something similar to what you do. Here is his card…" And she would go on to tell me all about her new friend.

On those trips to California, Mom and Dad loved to take the family out for dinner—to Koya's in Folsom, or Café LaSalle on Howe Av, or some other favorite restaurant. Archie used to joke that Mom could go to the ladies room and come out with a new friend to introduce to the family. There were no strangers; just potential friends.

When they moved to California, we would attend services at Mosaic Law and sit with Shirley and Archie. At the conclusion of a service, Shirley would spend the next twenty minutes introducing me to all of her friends. These were all the folks who sat in the right-front section of the synagogue. She'd say, "Bernie (or whoever), have you met my son-in-law Chuck Spooner?" It was a little embarrassing because we'd been members of Mosaic Law for a dozen years and within a few months, Shirley knew more people than I did.

Let's talk about strength. Some of you may not realize this, but my mother-in-law was a very strong person. When she made up her mind, it was "case closed." I was in Chicago for a conference sometime in the early 80's. The conference was way out in the suburbs somewhere. I had a rental car, so I drove over to Mom and Dad's home on Coyle Avenue for dinner the first two nights I was there. On the third day, I was talking to some of the guys at the conference and they hadn't seen much of Chicago. So we cooked up a plan to go downtown that night, have a nice dinner, and then hit some of the clubs on Rush Street. I called Shirley during our lunch break to tell her about these plans and she was not happy with this idea. I think she pictured four guys turned loose in Chicago, "getting wild" on Rush Street. She did not like that picture. So we talked a little longer and then she said, "No, you'll come over and have dinner with Dad and me. Why don't you plan to be here around seven."

So I went to Mom and Dad's around seven. If I remember correctly, we went to Fluky's for a hot dog.

But now, let's talk about *real* strength. In one of his recent High Holy Day sermons, Rabbi Taff raised three questions. Number one: what do you do in the time of your greatest joy? Number two: what do you do in the time of your greatest loss? And number three: what do you do in the time of your greatest testing? The answers to these questions speak volumes about a person's character.

Linda & Sid, Ron, Barbara and I were there to witness Shirley & Archie in the time of their greatest loss *and* their greatest testing. Many of you know that Shirley and Archie lost their son Michael to leukemia at the age of fourteen. I will never forget seeing the two of them—literally—holding each other upright at the cemetery on a bitter cold Chicago day.

A devastating loss. A terrible, terrible test.

That was in January, 1977. Not long after that, in one of those long, long talks that I was privileged to share with Shirley, she told me that she and Archie made a decision that they would live the rest of their lives in a way that would honor Mike's memory. And for the next three and a half decades, that's exactly what they did.

I've often wondered if I would have that strength, if I could stand that test. I don't know the answer, but I do know that I have—not one, but two—excellent role models.

Wise, funny, knowledgeable, informed. Kind, loving, generous, devoted to her family. Warm, friendly, and amazingly strong. That was my mother-in-law, Shirley Vine. May her memory be for a blessing.

Wonderful, Wonderful

I was browsing through the channel guide last Saturday and a program on PBS caught my eye: "Johnny Mathis – Wonderful, Wonderful." It had been a long, long time, so I thought I'd give him a listen. Sure enough, there was Johnny, looking his age if not older, the face fuller and deeply lined, the hair getting a little thin. And then there's that voice: a little deeper and darker now, but still with that unique tremulous quality that wraps so perfectly around a pretty ballad.

Johnny was singing "Stranger in Paradise" when I tuned in and I was struck by the lyrics. *If I stand starry eyed / That's a danger in Paradise / For mortals who stand beside / An angel like you.* They just don't write 'em like that anymore, do they? And I couldn't help but notice the urgency and passion in his delivery, as though he knows how much these old songs mean to us.

I'll bet there are some of you out there smiling right now, gazing off into the distance, remembering when that special someone was in your arms and you were saying your first I-love-you's, and there's Johnny on the car radio singing "The Twelfth Of Never." Or you're back in the first apartment you shared, up on the top floor looking out over the lights of the city, and you're marveling at how beautiful she looks dressed in candlelight, and Johnny is on the stereo singing "Wild Is The Wind." Or you're looking at your daughter, a grown woman now with teenagers of her own, and you start to say, "Did I ever tell you about the night you were conceived?" But you stop yourself, because that would be too much information. So you smile and say, "You know, I really love that song 'Misty'" and you let it go at that.

I wonder what music kids make out to today? Lady Gaga? 50 Cent? Katy Perry's "Teenage Dream?" I feel for 'em if that's all they've got. Maybe they skip the making out and—what's the saying?—just get busy. Sad thought.

I remember seeing Johnny live at the Minneapolis Auditorium in the early sixties. He was just a skinny young man then, but he held us in the palm of his hand for an hour and a half. After the show, I compared notes with a dear friend, born and raised in Iowa, and found that he too fell in love with Johnny singing in the background. Isn't that something? You could watch submarine races in California, or listen to the corn grow in Iowa, and there was one voice that touched us all.

Johnny Mathis was the soundtrack of our lives, an important part of it anyway. He was there with us in moments we'll never forget, and when you hear the songs again, it all comes back. Kids today don't know what they're missing. Our music was simply the best.

The Day Joe Came to Town

Vallejo Little League received its charter and held its first player draft in 1952. As I write this (April, 2012), the league has just celebrated its sixty-first opening day. That's a remarkable milestone, especially for those of us who were there for the first one. But the one many of us will never forget was opening day 1954.

That's the day Joe DiMaggio came to town.

Joseph Paul DiMaggio. Joltin' Joe. The Yankee Clipper. Thirteen seasons with the Yankees, thirteen times an all-star, and three times league MVP. Nine World Series championships. A lifetime .325 batting average. He of the venerable fifty-six game hitting streak achieved in 1941, arguably a record that will stand forever. The man who retired in 1951 at the relatively young age of thirty-seven because chronic injuries prevented him from playing like Joe DiMaggio.

He wouldn't give the fans anything less.

First, a little background. Vallejo Little League played its first two seasons at an all-dirt diamond located at Tennessee Street and Highway 40, on land owned by Ed Case of Ed Case's Minit-Man Car Wash. It's pretty remarkable to think of it now. There were four teams, fifteen players to a team, sixty kids in total for the entire city of Vallejo. That very first year, the post-season All Star team came within one win in Santa Monica of advancing to the World Series in Williamsport, Pennsylvania. But then Vallejo was a great baseball town, with talent developed on the sandlots under the recreation district program managed by Lyston Johnson. When you picked the best players from that talent pool, it's no wonder they were successful.

But that was 1952. In 1954, we were moving to our permanent home: Callen Field at the corner of Amador and Florida Streets. It was a diamond with real grass in the infield and outfield, grandstands on both sides, and a two-story building behind the backstop that would house a snack bar, equipment storage, a meeting room, and a press box. From that second story perch behind home plate, Ray Denny would broadcast our games live on the local radio station.

Opening day 1954 was an occasion to be celebrated. As it turned out, it was a day we would never forget.

Al Manfredi was a twelve year-old third baseman for Steffen's Sport Shop, one of the four sponsored teams in the league. (The other sponsors were Marine Chevrolet, Case's Car Wash, and The Optimist Club.) Al's father, a respected pharmacist and businessman, happened to be a friend of Dominic DiMaggio. Dom was known as "The Little Professor," one of the three DiMaggio brothers, along with Vince and Joe, to come out of San Francisco and play major league baseball. Mr. Manfredi would see Dom from time to time at the family's restaurant on Fisherman's Wharf. They were discussing Little League baseball one day and he asked Dom if Joe would consider coming to opening day ceremonies. Dom said he didn't know, but he would ask. About two weeks before opening day 1954, Mr. Manfredi received a call from Dom: "Joe says he will be there."

That didn't leave much time for planning, but I think everyone would agree that Joe made it as easy as possible. With teams lined up around the base lines and the stands packed with friends and family, he stood in the infield and made a few remarks. He posed for a picture with each team. He even posed for some small group and personal photos.

One of those shots included Ronnie Smith, Jerry Warren, and Bruce Bigelow of the Steffen's Sport Shop team. Bruce has that picture blown up and framed, sitting where everyone can see it in his home. Eddie Hewitt, who played for the Optimist Club, remembers a photo that appeared in the *Times-Herald* showing Joe holding a bat, giving batting tips to my teammate Steve Cox. Steve hit a homerun that day. I'll bet Steve held on to that picture, too.

Joe also sat for an interview that appeared in the *Times-Herald*. I can't remember if it was with Dave Beronio or Don Gleason, but it was a full column. Of course the interviewer had to ask the question that was on everyone's mind: "So, Joe, where is Marilyn?"

Joe and Marilyn Monroe were married in January of 1954, and their stormy relationship was still in the honeymoon stage. Joe's answer was that Marilyn was off making a movie. Checking her filmography, my guess is that she was shooting *There's No Business Like Show Business*, released in December 1954. Her next film would be *The Seven Year Itch*, which began production in September of that year, and included the famous scene of Marilyn standing on a subway grate, the wind blowing her skirt up over her head. The filming of that event reportedly made Joe furious and the couple had a horrendous fight as a result.

Marilyn filed for divorce a month later. The marriage lasted just nine months; or in Joe's case, for the rest of his life. It is the stuff of legend now. How they were rumored to be getting back together again, just before her death in 1962. How he claimed her body, took over the arrangements for her funeral, and kept it small, quiet, and dignified. How for twenty years, he had roses delivered to her crypt three times a week.

In 1967, *The Graduate* was released. It was the film that launched Dustin Hoffman's career and it included an evocative soundtrack by Simon and Garfunkle. One of the songs, "Mrs. Robinson," included the following lines:

> *Where have you gone, Joe DiMaggio*
> *Our nation turns its lonely eyes to you*
>
> *What's that you say, Mrs. Robinson*
> *Joltin' Joe has left and gone away*

I remember Joe being interviewed on television and being asked what he thought Paul Simon meant by those lines. Joe said, "Ya know, I have no idea."

I think he was being modest. We all knew what Simon was getting at. The war in Vietnam was at its high point, with more than five hundred thousand men and women deployed there. It was the age of the credibility gap—that vast disconnect between what we were being told at home versus what we could see every night on our television screens. Paul Simon was saying *where are our heroes? Where are the men and women of integrity? Where are the people we can count on?*

Funny thing: that was a long time ago, but the questions remain the same.

So here we are at opening day 2012. I wonder if Vallejo Little League had any special guests, and what words of encouragement they had to offer? I wonder how many kids were there in uniform, listening to the adults ramble on, itching to get the ceremony over with and the games underway? And I wonder what those kids—and the adults— would say if you told them that Joltin' Joe DiMaggio stood on Callen Field on its very first opening day in 1954?

I wonder…

The Best Laid Schemes

I was reminiscing via e-mail with my old friend, Jerry Warren, and the conversation turned to books. I mentioned that one of my favorites is John Steinbeck's *Of Mice and Men*. I haven't read it for a while, but the exchange with Jerry set me to thinking.

There is a scene in the book where George and Lennie, those quintessential itinerant farm workers, are sitting around the table in the bunkhouse talking about their dream: to own a place of their own. George even knows of a small farm that's available if only they could get the money together. Candy, the one-handed old man who works on the ranch, says he has some money saved and he'd be willing to throw in with them if they'd just let him live there and tend the chickens. George pencils it out and comes to the realization that together they can swing it. Their dream can become a reality.

It is an electric moment, one of the great ones in American literature, because it touches on a universal truth: everyman's dream of a home, a place to call his own, a piece of God's good earth. This is why, more than seventy years after it was published, *Of Mice and Men* still resonates with so many people. I'll admit that I am one of them.

It resonates for me because of my father. "Three or four acres in the Napa Valley," he would say. "That's what I'd like to have when I retire." Even in the early 1950s that dream was probably out of reach for a shipyard worker. And yet, I heard him say it over and over again.

We didn't have a car in our family until I was nine years old. We relied on city buses to get around town. Finally, in 1951, my dad decided it was time. My mom arranged for someone to give her driving lessons (my dad refused to drive because of a bad experience as a young man), and my parents negotiated a deal for a new Chevy sedan. Suddenly we had wheels! Not surprisingly, our favorite form of family entertainment was to take a Sunday drive, often with my older brother Dick behind the wheel. Most Sundays the destination was the Napa Valley, extending as far north as St. Helena and occasionally including side trips off Highway 29.

"Just three or four acres, Charlie. That's all a man would need." It was my dad's dream until the day he died.

There are many versions of *Of Mice and Men* out there for your viewing pleasure: the classic 1939 film version starring Burgess Meredith and Lon Chaney, Jr.; the 1970 television production with George Segal and Nicol Williamson; and the 1981 television version with Robert Blake and Randy Quaid. And every now and then your local theater company will stage a revival.

There are a couple of things to look for in judging any production of this classic. First, does it adhere to the Steinbeck original? It drives me nuts when a screenwriter or director has the unmitigated brass to rewrite John Steinbeck. Just look at what Davis S. Ward did to *Cannery Row* in his 1982 film version. There oughta be a law!

Second, how well do they perform that critical scene in the bunkhouse? They absolutely have to nail it because, after all folks, that's what it is all about. Say it with me: "Universal Truth."

Having set the criteria, let me recommend Gary Sinise's 1992 film version, starring Sinise as George and John Malkovich as Lenny. In my humble opinion, this movie gets it ninety percent right.

It always makes me think of my dad. And it always brings a tear to my eye.

Uncle Pat

There was a great commercial that ran during the recent (2012) baseball playoffs and World Series. Former Cubs pitcher Kerry Wood is walking along the ivy-covered outfield wall at Wrigley Field with a State Farm agent, talking about the "discount double-check." Kerry says he used to do an "ivy double-check" before home games, because people leave all kinds of things in the ivy. He reaches in and pulls out an old cell phone, a French horn, and—surprise—Andre Dawson, a Cubs star and Hall of Famer from the late-eighties.

I can envision my own version of that walk. I would reach into the ivy and out would come my uncle, Frank "Pat" Pieper, and George Herman "Babe" Ruth.

Uncle Pat was born in Hanover, Germany, in February of 1886. The family immigrated to the U.S. and settled in Denver. As a young man, Pat left home for Chicago to seek his fortune. He went to work for the Cubs organization in 1904, starting as a vendor at the West Side Grounds where the Cubs played their games. When the franchise was purchased and moved to what is now Wrigley Field in 1916, he became the field announcer.

The stadium was built in 1914 to be the home of the Chicago Federals in the old Federal League. It was originally called Weegham Park in honor of the Federals owner, Charles H. Weegham. When the Federal League folded in 1915, Weegham bought the Cubs franchise from the Taft family and moved them into Weegham Park. P.K. Wrigley purchased the club in 1920 and renamed the stadium Cubs Park. Finally, in 1926, it officially became Wrigley Field, also known as "the friendly confines" to us Cubs fans.

Uncle Pat's job was to announce the lineups, the batters, the defensive changes, and so on. One problem: Wrigley Field did not have a public address (PA) system until 1932. From 1916 until the system was installed, he made his announcements by way of a very large megaphone. I've seen pictures from those days captioned "Pat Pieper and his Pipes."

When the PA system was installed in 1932, Uncle Pat was given a small table near the backstop, behind home plate on the third base side. And that's where he worked until he was past his eightieth birthday and the club decided to move him to the press box for safety.

During his fifty-nine years as the Cubs announcer, he missed only sixteen games; none after 1924. His signature line, one that you would hear before every home game, was this: "Attention... attention please... have your pencils and scorecards ready and I'll give you the correct lineups for today's ballgame..." My wife Barbara grew up in Chicago attending games at Wrigley Field and she remembers the voice and that familiar phrase. She was back at the stadium for a game during the summer of 1975 and she realized that something had changed. It was later that she learned that Pat Pieper had passed away in October, 1974.

He is honored with a star on the Cubs Walk of Fame outside the ballpark. In the summer of 2002, I was in Chicago to visit my dear friends, Lee Nidetz and Moira Higgins, and to help them celebrate the ten-year anniversary of their consulting firm, Technology Staffing Resources, Inc. Part of that celebration was a trip to Wrigley Field to see the Cubs play the Giants. As we waited outside the stadium for our group to assemble, I found myself standing next to the Walk of Fame. Moira snapped a picture of me with Uncle Pat's star.

Now, what about Babe Ruth, the other guy that I pulled out of the ivy? Well, that brings us to the legend of the Called Shot Homerun.

It was the third game of the 1932 World Series, Cubs vs. the Yankees at Wrigley Field. Babe came to bat in the fifth inning, Charlie

Root on the mound for the Cubs. The Cubs bench was riding Ruth mercilessly, and the Babe was giving it right back to them. With two strikes, Ruth began to gesture with his right hand, a fact confirmed years later by the discovery of a home movie taken by Matt M. Kandle, Sr. Was Ruth pointing at the Cubs dugout? Was he pointing at Charlie Root? Or was he pointing to the center field wall, indicating that's where he would hit the ball? Whatever the case, he hit the next pitch an estimated 440 feet into the right center field bleachers. The Yankees won game three and then won game four to sweep the series.

A New York sportswriter, Joe Williams, was the one who coined the phrase "Called Shot." No one else but Mr. Williams seemed to notice. Babe Ruth didn't say anything about it for several days, but finally seemed to realize that it made for a great story. Did he really call his shot? There is testimony on both sides saying "yes he did" or "no he didn't." From my research, the consensus is this: we'll never know for sure.

But wait a minute. What about the field announcer, sitting back there by the backstop? What did Pat Pieper have to say? In an interview with the *Loveland (Colorado) Reporter-Herald*, given in June, 1971, this is what he said:

> Don't let anybody tell you the Babe didn't point to the bleachers before he slammed that homer off Charlie Root. I know, I had the best seat in the house. Babe shouted to Guy Bush, the Cub pitcher who was heckling him from the bench: 'That's two strikes, but watch this,' as he pointed to the right field stands. Root came in belt high with the next pitch and, wham, it was gone.

So, after all the experts have had their say and after all the eyewitnesses are long gone, what are we to believe? I don't know about you, but I think I'll go with Uncle Pat.

How to Buy a Senator

April 19, 2013

It was heartbreaking to listen to the parents of the children murdered at Sandy Hook Elementary in Newtown, Connecticut, pleading last week with senators to pass sensible gun control legislation. But with all due respect, they are going about it the wrong way. Instead of using common sense, logic, and appeals to human dignity they need to ask a simple question:

How much does it cost to purchase a vote in the Senate?

Here is my best guess: an average of $10 million ought to be enough. The key word there is "average." It should cost much less in states like Rhode Island or Delaware, leaving more money to spend in the big media states like Florida, Texas, and California. I know that $10 million multiplied by 100 senators is a lot of money. But how about this: just focus on purchasing the senators who are up for reelection in the coming election cycle. That means only thirty-three senators, more or less, requiring a mere $333 million in round numbers.

Given the Supreme Court's *Citizens United* decision, the process should be pretty straight forward. Form a Political Action Committee— call it something innocuous like Citizens for an Effective Senate (CES for short)—and begin raising funds. In round numbers, 127 million people voted in the presidential election of 2012. The polls tell us that upwards of 90% of the people support sensible gun control legislation, such as expanded background checks. But let's be conservative and say that only 70% of the 127 million will actually contribute to CES. That means if 88.9 million people contribute $3.75, CES will have its $333 million; they can then go about the business of purchasing senators.

You may ask why not collect $11.25 from those 88.9 million people and go out and buy all 100 senators. That is certainly a possibility. Perhaps Phase Two.

The methodology is well defined. If a senator up for reelection opposes CES's position, pour money into a campaign to defeat him or her. If a senator who favors CES is facing a tough challenge, spend the $10 million shoring up his/her campaign. Of course there are senators like Feinstein who are solidly behind gun control; she carried the assault weapons ban that was allowed to expire, and she hasn't faced a serious challenge for her Senate seat. No need to spend money on her reelection. Use those dollars elsewhere.

As the Brits say, "And there you have it." No more appeals to logic and human dignity. Just purchase the votes you need. After all, that's what the NRA does.

Collision Course

February 25, 2014

"I believe in the Church of Baseball."

That was Annie Savoy's famous opening line in the movie *Bull Durham*. I would not go that far, but those who know me know that I love almost everything about baseball. Why the qualification? Because there is one thing I have always hated about the game at the professional level: violent collisions at home plate where the base runner lowers his shoulder and bulldozes the catcher. As in Pete Rose – Ray Fosse in the 1970 All Star Game. As in Buster Posey nearly seeing his career ended in May, 2011.

Today my sports page tells me that Major League Baseball is implementing a new rule intended to eliminate these career-threatening collisions. Will MLB get it right in the first iteration? Probably not. But I'm encouraged that they are willing to try. Let the new rule evolve; it can only improve our beautiful game.

I'm no fan of Bud Selig. When he finally retires, the game will be better for it. That said, the implementation of this new rule will definitely be listed in the positive column of Bud's legacy.

Annie closes the movie with a quote from Walt Whitman: "I see great things in baseball. It is our game, the American game. It will repair our losses and be a blessing to us."

Amen to that.

A reader writes...

From: David DeLiema
To: Chuck

Chuck, do you have any idea why they made an exception for home plate? Is it something about its value, the most "important" base, and needing to break through against greater odds to score a run? The stakes are basically heightened at that moment. Is it about the catcher defending his home turf or the catcher having less agility (because of the pads) than infielders? I wonder what it was.

Do you have similar feelings about runners sliding into second spikes up? That sets in motion the gorgeous leap and swivel throw, in one elegant motion, to first. We probably wouldn't want to lose that! I guess you could point out that the slide into second is meaningful, and it just so happens the runner has cleats on his shoes, forcing the second baseman to jump over him.

From: Chuck
To: David

David, you have to keep in mind that baseball folks are not the sharpest tools in the shed. They (we?) tend to be hidebound, dyed-in-the-wool traditionalists. The old-timers see themselves as the keepers of the flame, charged with passing on "the way the game is played" to each new generation.

Somewhere around the turn of the twentieth century, a big strong catcher said *Hey, I'm wearing all this padding—mask, chest protector, cup, shin guards—I'm gonna block home plate and watch all these little dopes wreck their shins sliding into me. Ha!* Pretty soon all catchers were doing it and it became part of *the way the game is played.*

Then along came Tyrus Raymond Cobb, by all accounts a nasty individual, who said *Screw that! If you're blocking the plate, I'm gonna run your ass over.* This too caught on and was added to *the way the game is played.*

And so, thanks to the traditionalists, that is the way it stayed all through the years. And every time a serious injury would occur (witness Pete Rose crashing into Ray Fosse in the 1970 All Star game) and someone would suggest changing the rules, the keepers of the flame would scoff and spit and say: *You can't change baseball. That's the way the game is played.*

Which brings us to May 25, 2011, when an obscure player named Scott Cousins barreled into Buster Posey and destroyed his ankle. You can find a film clip of the collision on the Internet—if you have the stomach to watch it. One of the brightest young stars of the game was suddenly facing the end of his career, a career that promised to sell millions of season tickets, not to mention jerseys bearing the number

28, catcher's mitts, bats, batting gloves, jock straps, and other baseball paraphernalia. Finally, the keepers of the flame said *Damn, this could cost us a lot of money. We got an investment here. Maybe we should protect it.*

And so, finally, in 2014, we have a change to *the way the game is played.* Call it The Buster Posey Rule. The traditionalists (e.g., Angels manager and former catcher Mike Scioscia) will scoff and spit and adjust their cups and say it's a bad idea. So be it. As the Bedouins say, "The dogs may bark but the caravan moves on."

PS: I think we can also thank Mr. Cobb for the "high spikes" slide. But there are plenty of rules to protect the middle infielders. It's just a matter of interpretation and enforcement by the umpires. And I do love the pivot and leap at second base. It's one of the great things about *the way the game is played.*

From: David
To: Chuck

I almost can't believe we're talking turn of the twentieth century stuff. That feels old in baseball terms, for me at least, but it pales in comparison to other inherited cultural traditions—religious, political structures, ways of treating the environment—protected by the powers that be. The upshot, and the thing that'll keep me busy until my dying breath, is that we have to be assiduous in questioning when to revise and when to maintain. So much of our moral compass comes from within the traditions themselves, which often cause a lot of suffering (ranging from wrecked ankles to wars). The traditions are offered at some point in time, maintained for certain reasons at that point in time, and then appropriated over great stretches for potentially new reasons. If the moral compass comes from within the tradition, then you get nonsensical stuff like Scioscia arguing to allow a play misaligned with the rules of the game and the protection from equipment. From where, then, should our moral compass come, if not from carbon copies of the rules inherited in our traditions? Are there superorder values, commandments, intuitions? The golden rule? It's interesting to engage with these questions in well-defined contexts, like baseball, because even then you encounter a whole web of issues (the economics of the game, the safety of the players, the norms of the game, comparisons to the way other sports are played, retaliation, competitiveness).

What a stimulating piece. Thanks again!

From: Chuck
To: David

Wow! Very thought-provoking. You obviously see things in a much larger context. I, on the other hand, just hate seeing catchers mowed down at home plate.

I hope that we never fall into the fallacy of looking to MLB owners, or the Players Association for that matter, as keepers of our moral compass. Together they have visited more abuse on this great game and its fans then we would have the time or energy to list.

The fact that more than seventy million people attended a major league game last year is testimony to the enduring strength of baseball and its traditions. At its very roots, it is a game for fathers to pass on to their sons (or daughters). It is summed up in that iconic scene from the end of *Field of Dreams* when Ray Kinsela says, "Hey, Dad…wanna have a catch?" and they begin to toss a ball back and forth. That is what it's all about.

The saga continues…

It's October, 2015, and there on my TV screen Chase Utley (Dodgers) barrels into Ruben Tejada (Mets) at second base, breaks up a double play and breaks Tejada's leg. Meanwhile, a Dodger runner on third base scores. Utley is initially called out; he trots off the field without ever touching second base.

Is this good hard-nosed baseball, or an illegal play? Should the umpire have ruled it a double play (Rule 6.01 (6)) and sent the runner back to third, thereby preserving the Mets' one-run lead?

After viewing replays from all angles, the umpires decided thusly: Tejada was pulled off the bag at second by the throw; therefore, Utley was awarded the base in order to "make the play right," and the runner from third was allowed to score.

The next day, Joe Torre, Major League Baseball's chief baseball officer, announced a two-game suspension for Utley for sliding late. Torre defended the umpires, reminding us that they have to make decisions in an instant, a very difficult job. Utley and the Players Association immediately appealed the suspension, delaying its enforcement into the indefinite future.

I have great respect for Joe Torre, but he got it only partially right. Here is how it should have gone down: first, suspend the umpire for *not* enforcing Rule 6.01 (6), even with the advantage of video replay. Second, rule it a double play and send the runner back to third. Finally, rule that the game must be resumed from that point and played to completion.

I'm sure that such a ruling would violate a dozen clauses in the collective bargaining agreement, and raise the mother of all shit storms. But I can dream, can't I?

What about Chase Utley? I have always admired him and the way he plays the game. He was doing exactly what umpires have allowed over an extended period of time. The proof of this was in the numerous replays that the networks and highlight shows ran, showing recent late slides at second that were *not* penalized. Until the umpires enforce the rule, players are going to continue take out middle infielders with aggressive slides. Or rolling body blocks. Depends on your point of view.

Back to the real world, what Joe Torre and MLB need to do is this: clarify the rule to state that the runner must start his slide (i.e., hit the ground) before a line parallel to the base, *and* that he must attempt to occupy the base as a result of his slide. Failure to do either of those two things would result in the invocation of Rule 6.01 (6).

Baseball doesn't need middle infielders with broken legs. It needs clear rules and guidelines for its umpires. And it needs umpires who will enforce the rules.

We still have the World Series of 2015 to play. Any chance we can get this right?

Remembering Dillon

The facts are straight forward: "Dillon James Mini, 73, passed away on Monday (September 15, 2014) after a long illness." The obituary doesn't contain a lot of detail, but it doesn't need to. Not for me. For me, the details are all in my mind, like a shoebox full of old snapshots that you have promised to organize—someday. I am going to open that shoebox now and let them come tumbling out.

Here's one of Dillon and me walking down the Jennings Street hill, heading who-knows-where, maybe to my house down on Russell Street, or down to the playground at Steffan Manor. It's summer and Dillon just turned eight, and I'm six, looking forward to my seventh birthday in September. This was the day we swore to each other (probably a pinky swear) that we'd be best friends forever. We kept that vow for a long, long time.

Here's a picture of his dear parents, Dillon H. and Bernice. I remember the first time I knocked on their front door to ask if Dillon could come out to play. My orthodontist had fitted me with an elaborate headgear contraption that looked like a canvas helmet; it had a metal chin cup attached with rubber bands, and it was designed to pull my jaw back and correct a severe under-bite. Mrs. Mini answered the door and I think she was shocked to see me there, looking like a little alien. Over time, the Minis became second parents to me, and what beautiful people they were. Mrs. Mini was one of the all-time great cooks, at least in my book, and she loved feeding me. And Mr. Mini was always playful and funny, teasing me gently, making me laugh. I'm not sure why, but they liked me and treated me like a son, taking me along wherever they traveled.

Here is a good one. It's a picture of Bruce Bigelow with Dillon and me on the day Bruce moved into the neighborhood. Dillon and I saw him playing in the yard there on the corner of Buss and Russell, and we went over and introduced ourselves. Bruce was about eight at the time. It was the start of a three-way partnership that would last most of our lifetimes.

This next one is priceless. It is from the sports page of the *Times-Herald* and it's our City Championship baseball team – Underweight Division. There's Dillon with the catchers gear falling off his body, always too big for him; and Bruce, Jerry Warren, Andy Carlson, John O'Neil, Mike Kennedy, and of course, Jake Catado, our GVRD playground leader at Steffan. What a great guy! Jake, if you're reading this, you should know that we all loved you. But where is Roger Ashlock? He was part of that team, our ace pitcher.

God, what fun that was: hanging out down at Steffan, going out to the ball field to practice, traveling across town to play other schools. We'd pile into Jake's old Chevy, a dozen of us or more, and sing "99 Bottles of Beer on the Wall," or "John Jacob Jingleheimer Schmidt" all the way across town. It was pure fun. No pressure, no expectations, just the love of the game and each other.

Here is a great shot: Dillon, Bruce, and me on Little League opening day, 1952; Dill and Bruce wearing their Steffen's Sport Shop uniforms and me with Ed Case's Minit Men across my chest. It was the first Little League in Vallejo and we were part of a group of sixty kids that got it started. It was an experience none of us—Dillon, Bruce, Jerry, Roger, Frank Bodie, Eddie Hewitt, Joey Butler, Tom Case, Al Manfredi, Jim Eaton—I could go on and on—will ever forget. In fact, we still rehash the old play-by-plays when we get together.

This next picture makes me smile. There we are on somebody's lawn, surrounding a big, handsome collie named King. King belonged to Gary and Lennie Price and he had some sort of tumor that had to be removed. So we went out mowing lawns to raise money for the vet. Someone called the *Times-Herald* and we wound up on the front page. Several readers offered to pay for King's surgery so we didn't have to mow many lawns. Was the lawn mowing Dillon's idea? Or was it Roger's?

Later that summer, we all took a hike out to Blue Rock Springs, then up over the hills to the old abandoned mercury mines to go exploring. Gary fell down a mine shaft. He was lucky to survive. We never went hiking out there again.

This next one is a classic: Dillon in his football uniform at Hogan. Yeah, football. You see, Dillon was always small for his age. As an adult, he was maybe 5'6", 120 pounds. But in the ninth grade, he still had some growing to do. All of his young life, people would tell him "…you're too small to do that." Whether it was baseball, football, bowling—it didn't matter. So naturally he set out to prove them all wrong.

I remember going out to watch the team practice on the Hogan field. Bill McGrath was a tenth-grader, the star of the team, and he was built like a tank. Coach Pelligrini was running a drill where there were two lines about ten yards apart: ball carriers and tacklers. When you came to the front of the line, he'd toss the ball to the ball carrier who would take off running. The tackler's job was to bring him down. They had to stay in a narrow lane marked by two blocking dummies. It was bound to happen sooner or later, and sure enough, Bill and Dillon wound up facing each other, Bill the ball carrier, Dillon the tackler. They went at each other and Dillon hit Bill hard, just above the kneecaps. Of course, he just bounced off and Bill ran on through, but everybody who witnessed it came away with great respect for Dillon Mini. He had more guts than anyone out there.

Here's a picture of Dillon as student body president at Hogan in the tenth grade. He wrote a column for the school newspaper titled "Pres Sez," or something like that. If you had asked me then (1957), I would have predicted that Dill would have a career in politics. Prominent family name. Good looking guy. Intelligent. Great personality. He was a natural.

Here's another good one. It's our bowling team down at Miracle Bowl on Tennessee Street. We were all in high school at the time. Miracle Bowl sponsored us and the idea was that we'd travel around and bowl junior teams from other towns. There's Dillon, Bruce, me, and Buddy Whisenhunt. Buddy was a lefty and a terrific bowler. Bruce and I were just okay. The traveling team idea never jelled, but we had fun while it lasted. Dillon would go on to become one of the best bowlers in Vallejo. He had several three-game series in the 800s and his press clippings could fill a scrapbook.

Oh my, here's a stack of photos from Tahoe. In the early fifties, the Minis bought a cabin near the South Tahoe Y. They would always spend the last two weeks before Labor Day at the cabin, and they'd invite me join them. I treasure the memory of those summer days. Here we are trout fishing on the Upper Truckee River; playing miniature golf down by Bijou; exploring the woods behind the cabin; playing hours and hours of ping pong in the garage; and hanging out on the beach at Camp Richardson. And here are the Silveiras who eventually built a place up there: Manuel & Mildred, plus Marie, Mike, and Marty. What a great family, and what a dear friend Marie was. And here are Mr. and Mrs. Bradley with Jerry and Russ. We had a lot of fun with the Bradley boys.

One time Jerry Bradley Sr. checked us all into the movie theater at Harrah's. We were supposed to stay there until an adult checked us out. The movie stunk so we snuck out and hit the streets of Stateline—me, Dillon, Jerry, and Russ. (I think Marie was babysitting for Mike and Marty.) It was all cool until one of us decided to drop a quarter in a slot machine just inside the door of Harrah's. We got busted and they paged Mr. Bradley to tell him his kids were loose on the street. With firm conviction he said, "They are not! I put 'em in the movie myself." We caught a lot of flack over that one.

There are about a thousand pictures from Tahoe in my memory bank. We'll have to look at all of them sometime.

This next shot is a beauty. It is a picture of Dillon as a member of a wedding party. He looks great in the white dinner jacket and the black tux pants. What a handsome guy. Our friend Charlie Gebhardt sang at that wedding. I remember he muffed the first verse of "The Lord's Prayer" and had to start over. Dillon cracked up laughing. Charlie made it through on the second try without a hitch.

Here is a picture of Dillon putting out a For Sale sign in front of my mom's house in 1975. We had to move her into an assisted living facility and Dillon handled the sale. He was in the real estate business for a number of years, though I couldn't tell you exactly how many.

This next one hurts. It's a picture of Dill and me sitting on a couple of bar stools down at Teeters, a joint near Georgia Street and the freeway. The place eventually changed names but we kept our same old stools. Whenever I would drive through Vallejo, usually on the way to The City, I'd stop at Teeters to see Dillon. Nine times out of ten he was there. We would throw back a few tall cold ones and rehash all the good old times.

How stupid of me! Why didn't I jerk him off that stool and drag him out of there? Would it have made a difference? Would it have changed anything in the latter part of his life? I guess I'll never know. As my sons would say, "That's on you, Dad. You'll have to wear that one."

The next picture is bitter-sweet. A bunch of us got together to visit Dillon in the group home where he spent his days before he moved into hospice care. I think it was 2011. There we are: Jerry Warren, Roger Ashlock, Russ Sturgeon, Gordie Maki, Sargent Johnson, Dave Plump, and me. We took him to the Sardine Can for lunch. I think he really enjoyed getting out with the guys. He was able to walk, slowly, with a walker, and he smiled and laughed and conversed with all of us, at least a little. I hope it was a good day for him.

Here are a few pictures I'd like to erase. On my last visits with him, he was barely able to walk, and our conversation consisted of his one-word responses to my questions. It was just a matter of time.

Ah, now this last picture is real. It's not just in my mind. It shows Dillon bowling, at the foul line delivering the ball, rolling what I'm sure was a sledgehammer shot to the 1-3 pocket. Yes, I know the photo is old and battered, but I want you to see it through my eyes. Look at the form. Look at the concentration. You can almost feel the fire in his belly. He was some competitor, my friend Dillon. And there he is at the very top of his game.

This is the way I will remember him. He was beautiful. Wasn't he?

Augie 'n Me

I am a die-hard baseball fan and one of the things I look forward to every June is the College World Series (CWS) played in Omaha, Nebraska. It is a chance to see the most talented players in the nation perform on a national stage. ESPN's coverage has expanded and improved year after year and helped to grow the popularity of the college game. And, I have to say that one of the things I look forward to each year is to see Augie Garrido's smiling (or serious) face on my television screen.

Augie has coached teams to fifteen CWS appearances, winning the championship five times—three with the Cal State Fullerton Titans and twice with the Texas Longhorns. With more than 1,900 victories, spanning five decades, he is the winningest coach in NCAA history. And, at age seventy-five, he isn't through yet. Even if the Longhorns are not in the tournament, Augie is generally there in Omaha as a spectator and always ready for an on-camera interview. He is wise, articulate, insightful, and certainly nobody can question his qualifications.

I think it is pretty darn cool: August Edmun Garrido, Jr., from Vallejo, California, is the winningest coach in college baseball history.

Batboy to the Stars
Growing up in Vallejo, my friends and I were well aware of Augie Garrido. He had a reputation as a slick fielding infielder and a fiery competitor (some would say "hot head"), and he played with and against some of the legends of the Vallejo sports scene, including Norm Bass, Larry Himes, Clyde Huyck, Adney Bowker, and Lee Cook. American Legion Post 550 listed those guys on its roster in the summer of 1956. If there is a team picture around, it likely includes Mike Huyck and me because we were the team's official batboys.

That's right: I shagged bats for Garrido, Himes, Bass, and company, arguably one of the best legion teams in Vallejo history.

Augie played his college ball at Fresno State for Coach Pete Beiden, including a trip to the CWS in 1959. He went on to play in the Cleveland Indians organization from 1961 through 1966, rising as high as Triple-A Portland in the Pacific Coast League. He began his college coaching career at San Francisco State in 1969 and the rest, as they say, is history.

The Chunky Righthander

I had experienced some success as a kid ballplayer through my years in Little League and Jr. Peanut League, primarily as a pitcher. Then, at the beginning of the season when I was a sophomore at Vallejo High (1958), I strained a tendon in my right forearm which caused me to miss most of that year. The arm healed and I pitched a little the following year, but the old zip just wasn't there. Before the start of the 1960 high school season, I went to Coach Dick Biama and told him I didn't want to pitch anymore, that I'd prefer to compete for a starting position in the outfield. He agreed at the time, but when practice started in February, he and Coach Norm Tanner talked me into giving it one more try.

I'm glad they did because I had a successful season, highlighted by a shutout win against our arch rival Saint Vincent Hilltoppers, a team that included Hank McGraw and Mike "The Chief" Delgado. It was a nice way to wrap-up my "career" as an Apache.

Then it was on to the summer American Legion season and we went into it with high hopes. Our infield included Joe Rapisarda at first base, Mike Taylor at second, Dallas Roundtree at short, and Mike Huyck at third. Hank McGraw joined us for the summer and I was thrilled that I didn't have to pitch against him anymore. Our pitching staff included Billy Himes, Jim Tell, Al Lehman, Jerry Sax, Jim Owens, and me. Gary Basque and Milt Howton shared the catching duties. Stan McWilliams was our coach and we had great respect for his professional career and his knowledge of the game.

Take a look at the list of names above. Quite a few of them are members of the Vallejo Sports Hall of Fame, and deservedly so. As I said, we had high hopes.

In spite of the expectations, it was a disappointing summer for me. I did not pitch well and I moved steadily down the list of starting pitchers. Billy Himes, the "Cocky Little Lefty" as we called him, moved into the role as our ace. The other guys stepped up, and of course, everyone could see the great talent that Jim Owens possessed.

And so we played on through the summer, pointing toward our usual showdown with a team from the Sacramento district. If we beat the Sacramento team, we would move on to the California State Legion Tournament, to be held that year at Billy Hebert Field in Stockton. We eventually won that showdown and it was on to Stockton. But before we hit the road, there was the Alumni Game to be played.

The Alumni Game

One of Post 550's traditions was to schedule an annual Alumni Game, bringing back players from years past to play against the current team. In 1960, the alumni team would feature Augie Garrido. Augie had put up great numbers that year for Coach Beiden. If memory serves, he hit well over .400, and we all knew that he would go on to play professional ball.

Our plan for the game was that each member of our pitching staff would throw an inning or two. When it was my turn, I went down to the bullpen expecting nothing more than a routine outing. I was surprised as I started to warm up, because suddenly everything was clicking. There was pop and hop on the fastball and—wonder of wonders—the curve ball was breaking sharply and I was putting it in the strike zone, something I'd always struggled with.

You can call it being "in the zone" or whatever you want, but I knew this had happened to me only a handful of times through all the years that I had played baseball. I'm sure athletes in other sports experience it as well: in tennis, your serve becomes a rocket and your ground strokes are crisp and accurate; in golf, you hit every shot flush and all the putts are center-cut; in bowling, you find the perfect line and your ball hits the pocket like a sledgehammer. It is a rare and wonderful feeling and I had it that day.

I don't remember much about the situation when Augie came to bat, but I don't think any runners were on base. I decided to throw him mostly curve balls because I knew he'd seen far better fastballs than mine. I got a couple of curves by him for strikes, but eventually the count went to 3-and-2. Then I gave him a steady diet of curves, which he kept fouling off. I don't remember how many pitches I threw to Augie; it could have been ten, maybe more. Finally, I decided on a fastball low and away, hoping I could sneak it by him. It was a little farther outside than I wanted, but Augie reached out and hit a line drive between first and second base.

Yep, I gave up a line drive base hit to an outstanding hitter. End of story.

Hanging 'em Up

We finished fourth that year in the State Legion Tournament, after losing our first game to Fresno and their ace Wade Blasingame. Wade went on to have great early success in the majors with the Milwaukee/Atlanta Braves.

I played one more season for Coach McWilliams at Vallejo JC, a season in which I got hit so hard it made my ears ring. It was time to hang 'em up.

I began this story by telling you how much I enjoy the College World Series, and how I look forward to seeing Augie Garrido every year. Part of my enjoyment is thinking back to that Alumni Game. Does Augie remember Charlie Spooner and our little battle in the summer of 1960? I'm sure the answer is a resounding *no*. But I will never forget it. It was the last time I really felt like a pitcher.

II.

Assorted Poems...

NUKE: Ohhh…I've heard about stuff like this.
ANNIE: Yeah? Have you heard of Walt Whitman?
NUKE: No. Who's he play for?

-Nuke LaLoosh and Annie Savoy,
Bull Durham

The City I Remember

San Francisco, city of my endless childhood fantasies
City of St. Francis, Baghdad by the Bay
Before Baghdad was a dirty word
Howard Pease novels—*Foghorns, The Tattooed Man, Shanghai Passage*
Great ships anchored on the bay, waiting for a berth at the Embarcadero
Shining white city of bridges and hills and cable cars
Don't call it Frisco!

San Francisco, city of Christmas memories
Salvation Army bell ringers at every store
A pocketful of pennies to drop in their kettles
Magnificent Christmas trees at the Emporium and City of Paris
Union Square—the most beautiful store windows in the world
Lunch at Moore's Cafeteria
Watching the crowd turn the cable car on Powell
Stand back, folks, let's roll it forward now.

San Francisco, city of heroes
16th and Bryant—there used to a ballpark right here
Where have you gone, Joe DiMaggio?
The Giants at Candlestick
Say Hey Willie Mays, Stretch McCovey, Juan Marichal, Will The Thrill
The Warriors at the Cow Palace
Al Attles, Nate The Great Thurmond, Rick The Greyhound Barry
The 49ers at Kezar Stadium
Y.A. Tittle, Hugh McElhenny, Joe The Jet Perry, R.C. Alley Oop Owens
The fans waiting, praying, keeping the faith
Hoping that Walsh and Montana, Posey and Bumgarner
will come along—someday.

San Francisco, city of movements
Beatniks dressed in black, shouting poetry in the coffee houses
Ginsberg, Kerouac, Ferlinghetti, the City Lights Bookstore
Hippies in the Haight-Ashbury, the summer of love
Tune in, turn on, drop out
Gays in the Castro, coming out, demanding to be heard
Harvey Milk with his bullhorn, Dan White with his gun
Parade upon parade, protesters taking to the streets
Stop the war, free Huey, gay pride, free speech, we shall overcome
What do we want? You name it! When do we want it? Now!

San Francisco, city of tourists
I've got the camera, Mabel, let's see the sights
Catch the Powell & Hyde car at the turntable
Jump off at California Street
Meet me at the Top of the Mark
That's one expensive cocktail, Mabel
Jump off at Mason and Washington
Here's the car barn, look at that bull wheel!
Jump off at Lombard, crookedest street in the world
Look down the Hyde Street hill, God what a view
Jump off at the Buena Vista
Best Irish Coffee in the world, Mabel
Two over here, barkeep
Hey, how do we get to Chinatown?

San Francisco, city of great food
Ernie's and Paoli's, The Domino Club
Seafood at the Tadich Grill, Scoma's on the Wharf
North Beach, the aroma of garlic, butter and olive oil
The North Beach Cafe, Fior d'Italia
Filet of sole at the Washington Square Bar & Grill
(the Washbag to its friends)
The great ones fade, replaced by bright new stars.

San Francisco, city with a voice
Don Sherwood, Carter B. Smith, Al Jazzbo Collins, Dan Sorkin
KSFO, the world's greatest radio station
"The Sounds Of The City," world's greatest promo
Herb Caen, dot dot dot—must read him every day
Stanton Delaplane, Charles McCabe
Russ Hodges, "Bye bye, baby"
Lon Simmons, the voice of every team
Bill King, master of the microphone
The great ones are gone, they can never be replaced.

San Francisco, city of music
Miles Davis at the Black Hawk
Cannonball Adderley at the Jazz Workshop
Standing room only at the Fillmore
Joplin and Hendrix and The Dead
Sly Stone giving birth to funk
Different strokes for different folks
Pavarotti and Domingo rockin' the Opera House
Tony Bennett and Ella Fitzgerald at the Venetian Room
No wonder he left his heart.

San Francisco, city of sin
Crowds lined up outside Finochio's
Mabel, are you sure those are men?
Topless clubs strung out along Broadway
Bottomless waiting in the wings
The Chi Chi, Big Al's, The Condor, El Cid
Carol Doda and her twin 44s, Jill St. Paul totally nude
Hey buddy, come on in, sit right down front
Bring the girlfriend, you'll hold hands, you'll fall in love
Just a two-drink minimum
No cover (know what I mean?)

San Francisco, city of street people
Mimes and jugglers, musicians and peddlers
The Human Jukebox
The guy who sang calypso at Ghirardelli Square
The one playing "Star Eyes," channeling Charlie Parker
Homeless people in every doorway, on every heating vent
Streets reeking of urine and vomit
Toothless, eyeless panhandlers in your face
"Hey mister, spare change? Can you help a vet?
Walkin' on by? Well screw you too!"

San Francisco, city of my enduring dreams
City of St. Francis, Baghdad by the Bay
Shining white city of bridges, hills, and cable cars
Don't call it Frisco!
How beautiful you are—through the eyes of memory.

Regatta

c. 1956

At first they came in ones and twos
Then a dozen or so, and then
A flock, a gaggle, a hundred more

Carving their way out of San Pablo Bay
Tacking hard past The Lighthouse
Hell-bent for the Vallejo Yacht Club

Mainsail white and spinnaker blue
Hearty crewmen leaning far out
Riding the wind in a quiet rush

Paint it on the canvas of your mind:
The bridges and the *Golden Bear*
The Lighthouse and the breakwater

Houses on stilts along Sandy Beach Road
And a hundred boats a-racing
Regatta—Day Two—Fisherman's Wharf to Vallejo

There are few things so achingly beautiful
So exquisitely perfect
As a swift boat under full sail

The View

From the balcony of Building 50
High above the Berkeley campus
He looks out on the most amazing view.

On a clear fall night, not a trace of fog
And a full moon hanging over
The north tower of the Golden Gate,

A river of moonlight runs out
Across the bay to the Berkeley shore
The City off to the left, bathed in the glow.

A crown of lights rings the Top of the Mark
A bright white shaft marks the elevator
That reaches the Crown Room at the Fairmont.

Further left, the Bay Bridge and a steady line
Of taillights streaming into San Francisco
Leaping from Oakland to Yerba Buena and beyond.

It was a time when anything was possible
When the world stretched out before him
Much like that incredible view.

Can it be that he took it all for granted
That he thought it would be too easy
And all his mistakes would be forgiven?

What he wouldn't give to stand there again
The late-sixties and all those opportunities
Still waiting to be taken.

Now he closes his eyes to see that view
The moon, the bridges, the panorama spread below
And it reminds him of what might have been.

Close Encounter

A pile of dirty rags
A handmade sign
"Homeless, hungry, anything helps"
Is there a person in there?

Oh God, the pile just moved!
It's a woman
And a child
Kid can't be more than four.

How does this happen
Under our noses
While we're busy watching Caitlin
Keeping up with the Kardashians?

Is it drugs, abuse, alcohol?
Or guys like me
Who don't give a damn?

What's in my wallet?
Some ones... a fin...
"Here, here's a sawbuck
Make sure it goes for food."

She looks up, eyes vacant
Seeing through me
Her lips move
"God bless you."

I feel better now, moving on
Why am I walking so fast?
I could really use a drink
Where did I park the Lexus?

A pile of dirty rags
A handmade sign
"Homeless, hungry, anything helps"
Is there a person in there?

Like Brothers

He staggers out of the men's room
Weaving between the pool tables
Looking tiny and frail
His summer suit wrong for the season

He doesn't recognize me at first
Then his face lights up
Hey, been a long time
How the hell are ya?

I buy a round
(Am I an enabler?)
And we have the conversation
We've had a dozen times before

Remember that time
Down at Lemon Street
When you fell in the bay
Remember?

Remember the hike
Out to Blue Rock Springs
When Gary fell in the mine
Remember?

Remember we were City Champs
Underweight division
Jake was our coach, Roger our ace
Remember?

Remember all the guys
What a neighborhood we had
The best place at the best time
Remember?

Remember summers up at Tahoe
The beach at Camp Richardson
Fishing the Upper Truckee
Remember?

I loved your parents
They were the greatest
Treated me like a son
Remember?

What about yours
Great people too
Your mom drove us everywhere
Remember?

Another round, and then
We'll call it a night
I'll drive you home
My car's right outside

I drive up the hill
To the house where he grew up
So immaculate then
Crumbling now

Thanks, buddy, good to see ya
Give me a call, okay?
We guy-hug in the car
Our foreheads touch and linger

I watch him stagger up the walk
He falls flat, then bounces up
Damn, why didn't I walk him
Safely to his door?

Tomorrow he'll do it again
And the day after that
A short and vicious circle
With one dead certain end

Growing up together
Sharing our childhood
We were like brothers
Remember?

Requiem for Borders

The house of books stands empty
Its shelves are barren now
Where once the coffee bar did thrive
No tables mark the row.

The readers and the music fans
The kids at story time
Have drifted off to other shops
To spend their precious dime.

Whither now the printed page
In the age of Kindle and Nook?
And how can I e'er download
The smell of a brand new book?

Haitian Lullaby

January, 2010

Death and devastation around every corner
Bodies piled randomly in the streets
The face of pain etched forever in our minds
Brought to our family rooms in high definition

I wonder what it's like to be a victim
To have Katie Couric hold your hand
To see your pain mirrored in Diane Sawyer's eyes
To hear Anderson Cooper ask
"Where is your house?
What happened to your family?"

Giant planes land at the airport
Great ships anchor off the coast
Laden with food, water and medicine
Rescue teams and doctors from around the world
Brave people come to help—again

And now the hard part
The one that vexes us again and again
From Sumatra to New Orleans to Port-au-Prince
Moving what is needed to the people who need it
If only it was as easy as moving a camera crew

CBS, NBC, ABC, CNN, BBC, et al
Soon the proud logos will depart
To New York, to Washington, to London
Back to you in the studio, Katie
The 24-hour news cycle must be fed

On the island of Hispaniola
The face of pain remains
For the people of Haiti
Now becomes forever

Ode to Walmart

I cannot shop at Walmart
To do so takes panache
To devise a silly costume
Perhaps to show your ass

Or at least some sagging cleavage
Or multi-colored hair
A funny hat, or rolls of fat
To show you have a pair

I cannot shop at Walmart
The greeters turn me 'round
And send me off to Macy's
In another part of town

Chris

Don't do it, Chris.
Not today
not while the sun is shining
and spring is in the air.

Think about it, Chris.
Sleep on it
wake up tomorrow and watch
the sun climb the eastern sky.

One more day, Chris.
Tough it out
see the buds burst open
on the trees that line the street.

Then one more day, Chris.
Stay the course
until the days become weeks
and months turn into years.

Easy to say, Chris.
Suck it up
and all the other useless clichés
we use to fake the courage we do not feel.

Too late now, Chris.
Decision's made
executed before we knew it
sirens wailing, grim-faced cops at your door.

Where were we, Chris?
With helping hands
rather than empty words
when you needed us the most?

Here we are, Chris.
A day late
blaming God for being asleep on the job
when we're the ones who saw but did not act.

Author's note: Chris took his own life on April 4, 2011. He was seventeen years old.

Ed & Cindy

Beautiful!

That's the word that comes to mind
When I see them together
Pretty woman, handsome guy
A beautiful couple.

Who knew this would happen
Fifty-something years ago
When they'd pass in the hall at school
And—maybe—say "Hi!"

They've both lived meaningful lives
Lives of hard work and accomplishment
Filled with love, family, faith
Joyous wins, devastating losses.

And now what?
What wondrous adventures lie ahead?
I look at them and think
Maybe it's true after all
70 *is* the new 50.

Beautiful!

A Thousand Prayers

I'll bet we've said a thousand prayers
And then a thousand more
For you our dearest Kwajmom
No one deserves them more.

And what if they go nowhere
If no one out there hears
We pray and pray to an empty sky
Just to calm our fears?

No matter, we'll just pray some more
A thousand prayers, and then
Hold you with our loving thoughts
Till you're in our arms again.

Deanna

A gust of wind stirred the shade
That covers the bedroom window
Just enough to rattle the sash
And wake me from a restless sleep
One random burst, and it was gone

What weather event could cause
This errant surge of air
But then I thought of Deanna
Just forty miles away
Her head resting on a pillow
Her eyes closed to the world

We stopped in just last night
To say "We love you" one last time
"I love you too," she replied
Her spirit bright and still alive
In a body that's forsaken her

Could it be that she had passed
And this odd gust of wind
God's way to tell the world
And wake me to say one last prayer
For our beloved Deanna

Merry-go-round

Once more round, once more round
Let me ride again
The merry-go-round is slowing down
Why can't I ride again?

And shouldn't there be a brass ring
And shouldn't I be reaching
Is there a lesson here to learn
A message for the teaching?

Time was when you were with me
Upon this merry ride
Hands clasped on separate ponies
Together we would fly

Now the music's faded
The horses slow their pace
The crowd has closed around you
A shadow hides your face

Once more round, once more round
Help me understand
If I would go just once more round
Why won't you take my hand?

Seasons of Life

It has been a cruel season,
too many losses, too many funerals
too many times holding the shovel
waiting to cover another coffin.

Then again, we're at that age
as are those we love
the matriarchs, the patriarchs
the very foundation of our lives.

My great nephew, barely one year old
lets out a happy shriek
a cry that says, "I'm HERE, and it's GRAND
and I will NOT be ignored!"

God bless him
in all his beautiful blue-eyed wonder
for reminding us of dividends delivered
that Life renews and goes rolling on.

Timber Cove

Just above Ft. Ross, along the rocky coast
there's a place that is special to me
where the highway bends to embrace
a lovely ocean cove.

The path down to the narrow beach
is deeply cut and worn
for divers, fishermen and lovers
know this place so well.

A great rock sits at water's edge
its base washed by a stream
that flows from a redwood canyon
wound deep into the hills.

Beside that tumbling stream
hand in hand with those I love
sunlight through the redwoods high above
I've walked in God's cathedral by the sea.

Dream Weaver

What happens to the pieces
Of dreams that fall apart
Especially when you know
They grew within your heart?

Give them to The Weaver
To fix those broken things
To stitch them all together
And see what joy it brings.

Alas, there's no such person
To take this awesome task
Broken dreams stay broken
No matter whom you ask.

Best to build some new dreams
Perhaps on firmer ground
You're older now and wiser
They cannot take you down.

And still I cannot do it
I don't know where to start
For I still love the old dreams
The ones within my heart.

Pensacola Lost Bag Blues

(To the tune of "St. James Infirmary Blues")

I went down to the Saca'menna airport
For to catch me a southbound plane
Gave my bags to the airline man
I'll never see them again

Destination Pensacola
Two stops 'long the way
Who knows where my bags went
They done gone astray

(Chorus)
Let 'em go, let 'em go, God bless them
Wherever they may be
They may search this wide world over
They'll never find my bags for me

Now I can't change my skivies
Can't even shave my face
You know I'll need a change of sox
Before I leave this place

If you go down to the airport
Here's my advice to you
Cram your bag in the overhead bin
Carry that sucker with you

(Chorus – once more with feeling)
Let 'em go, let 'em, God bless them
Wherever they may be
They may search this wide world over
They'll never find my bags for me

Boomer's Lament

Retired.
It's a hard word to say
Even harder to swallow
So hard that I made up a term:
"Quasi-retired"
Isn't that cute?

It means if my old colleagues
Launched a mega-project
One with my special skill set
Written all over it
I'd go back in a flash
Arriving early, staying late
And loving it.

The months have flown by
I've stayed in touch
An email here, a phone call there
Dropping by just to say "Hi"
My way of saying
"Hey, look, I'm still here!"

Slowly the realization dawns
If that perfect project came along
My friends would likely say
"Let's get someone *like* whatshisname"
—or worse yet—
"Let's get a *young* whatshisname."

It's time to say it out loud
Time to drop the "quasi"
Old whatshisname is
Retired.

Persistence of Memory

December 18, 2012

How long will we remember
twenty dead children
and six dead adults
in a place called Newtown?

Will we remember the killer
and forget the victims?
Will we sing Auld Lang Syne
and simply move on?

God knows we've done it before—
Columbine, Virginia Tech, Aurora
Name the victims?
Sorry. Can't recall.

Picture the well-equipped first-grader:
Backpack, pencil box, ruler,
an apple for the teacher,
and a tiny Kevlar vest.

God help us if we forget.

Jason

You see him along the parkway
strolling casually toward Town Center
filthy clothes, wild hair, unshaven.

He is a young man named Jason
perhaps the same age as your sons
and you're sure that he lives somewhere
in the canyon, beside the muddy creek.

You see him in the market, buying a few
meager items of food, or in the bookstore
sitting in the café, a coffee cup in hand
staring through the window.

You see him at the bagel shop, sitting
in the sun on the patio, gazing into space
and you wonder how he came to this
and if there is a way that you can help.

You ask if you can get him something—
a sandwich, a drink, a burger and fries?
No thanks, he says, I'm fine, and then
he smiles a gentle smile.

When the storms roll in and the rain
pounds like a machine gun on your skylight
you say a prayer for Jason
in the canyon, beside the muddy creek.

Orange County

Spring, 2015

1.

Off to the gym again this morning.
Got to keep at it, to fight the steady
waning of strength and stamina.
The golf ball lands closer and closer
to where it took flight. It's neither the club
nor the ball. Merely the player.
Once I looked in the mirror and saw
A World Class Jock, able to master
any sport I chose. Now there is someone
different staring back, an old, tired-looking
gray-haired dude. A World Class *Altacocker.*
So it's off to the gym again this morning
where there's a treadmill with my name on it.
Artificial walking for a former jock.

2.

A beautiful sunrise over the Saddleback Range,
another sunny day in store, eighty-five degrees
in March. Pity those poor folks back East
with snow up to the eaves, snowplows fighting
to keep the streets passable, while in the OC
our concern is to apply the right sunblock.
Three hundred sunny days a year,
that's what my son Matt promised
when we decamped for Southern California.
In reality, it's more like three hundred forty.
I think I'll wear my new shorts today.

3.

Samantha sings "Castle on a Cloud"
and tears fill my eyes. The joy and love
I feel can't be contained, at least not
without a tissue. How did this little one,
with barely twenty-eight months practice,
wrap her tiny fingers so completely
around my heartstrings? It's a magic
trick I'll never understand, but
somehow she knows: she's got me.
God willing, she'll never let go.

4.

Out to retrieve the newspaper this morning,
the sun just beginning to peek over the
eastern ridge. The air is crisp and for a moment
I consider a nice long walk to start the day.
The thought passes as I remember the coffee
brewing in the kitchen and the comfortable
couch with my butt print imbedded upon it.
There will be plenty of time for walking
after I digest the Sunday *Register*, that faithful
chronicle of conservative Orange County, defender
of individual freedom and the right to *keep it all*.
Let all those freeloading tree-hugging illegal
immigrant Cadillac welfare queens earn their own.
Remind me to dust my portrait of Richard Nixon
and write a letter to the editor praising
Dick Cheney as a damn fine president.

5.

Much talk about heroes these days –
who is one, who is not, how do you judge?
Chris Kyle's name comes up, thanks to a movie
called *American Sniper*. Michael Moore
tells us that snipers are cowards. He lost a relative
to one in WWII, so he is quite certain, righteously
indignant, as only Michael Moore can be.
But aren't snipers simply weapons of war,
just like hundreds of other weapons systems?
Some are designed to kill millions of souls at a crack,
the innocent along with the guilty. Let God sort 'em out.
The crew of the *Enola Gay* flying toward Hiroshima:
Heroes or not? Like Harry Truman, you make the call.
Weapons—snipers included—should be spared the debate.
It is only the cause that can be judged, and then
only by the victor in the final battle.

6.

There are only five things to pursue in this life:
Love, beauty, compassion, justice, and a job.
Minus those elements, life doesn't amount to much.
Justice is where the fault lines exist, where we divide
into tribes to build our fortresses and our armies,
where we seek to smite our perceived Amalekites.
"Do not forget it!" Isn't that what God commanded?
(It depends on whose God is commanding.)
Justice rests in the hands of our leaders,
our patriotic duty: to get in line and send our
sons and daughters to enforce today's decrees.
Tomorrow's justice may wear a different face,
then what will yesterday's sacrifices mean?
We are left with love, beauty, compassion,
and the hope that we can pay our damn bills.

7.

Someone mentions a name
and suddenly it is 1957 again,
ninth grade, fourteen years old,
your fuzzy flattop slicked back
on the sides with Dixie Peach.
The sky was the limit then,
nothing beyond your reach.
You could move like the wind
and leap to touch the rim
given a running start.
That was the year you read
Great Expectations in English class,
when all the guys underlined that
famous line: "All of our intercourse
did pain me." Thank you, Mr. Dickens.
Did it all really happen the way
you remember it? Or is your memory
as fuzzy as that flattop?

8.

It's Spring again, or nearly so,
time for ballplayers to migrate
to Florida or Arizona for training.
Hope springs eternal through March,
every team in first place, for now.
It's time to find my copy of *Bull Durham*
and watch it for the thousandth time.
There should have been a sequel,
Bull Durham Redux. Crash makes it to
The Show as a manager; Nuke returns
as his pitching coach; Annie & Crash are
married with children. Too bad we couldn't
sell the idea to Ron Shelton. Then again,
it's better to quit while ahead,
Like *Hoosiers*, or *Breaking Away.*
Can you picture *Hoosiers II,* or
Breaking Away – Again?
And yet, Annie Savoy was right:
Crash would have been a fine manager.

9.

I love my little pill box
with its snap lid compartment
for every day of the week.
It was easy when I only took
one or two pills a day,
but now the count is up
to five or six. I get confused.
Ah, but my pill box keeps score
reminding me what to take
and when. Who invented this
ingenious tool? (Wish it were me.)

10.

It's Sunday evening again
and I'm waiting anxiously
for the *Monday Update* to arrive—
all those pictures and stories,
and news of old friends,
perhaps a verse from Mr. Collins,
the ARA from John Parks,
even a photo of Hank McGraw!
And through it all rings
the voice of Harry D,
the tie that binds, crusader
for righteous causes, his heart
on his sleeve, his checkbook
in hand. Where would we be
without him? I know Sunday
evenings would never be the same.

Babysitters
a.k.a. Bootcamp for Grandparents

Hush little baby, don't you cry
You've been fed and burped and changed
What could be wrong to make you sob so?
Look at those tears! Oh my God!
Try walking, try singing, try bouncing, try shushing
Maybe she's still hungry, try another bottle.

She's inconsolable, nothing helps
We are utter failures as grandparents
How did we ever raise children?
It's a miracle they survived
Whatever skills we had are long gone.

Oh wait—
The shushing seems to be working
Along with the bouncing…walking…singing
Oh my—
She's gone limp in my arms
I think she's asleep.

You know what, we've still got it
Like riding a bicycle, you never lose it
Look at that sweet little face
Have you ever seen anything so exquisite?
Where's the camera?
We have to get a picture of this!

III.

Reviews...

A few of my favorites.

Gentle Irreverence

Fated
S.G. Browne
New American Library, 2010

Rule #1: Don't get involved.

So says Fate, known as Fabio to all of his colleagues. Fabio is our narrator for this tale of what happens when you break the rules, especially considering who made them. Fabio is one of the Immortals, part of God's staff that includes Destiny, Death, the Deadly and Lesser Sins, the Intangibles, the Emotives, the Attributes and the Heavenly Virtues. Of course, our God Jehovah, known to the staff as Jerry, controls the big picture. The only thing I would have asked for to increase my enjoyment of this book is an organization chart, just so I could keep all the Immortals straight.

Fated is S.G. Browne's second novel, his first being the much-praised *Breathers*. *Breathers* is moving down that long, winding road toward becoming a movie. At last report, Diablo Cody of *Juno* fame is attached to the project. And, Browne's third novel, *Lucky Bastard*, will be published this year by Simon & Shuster. It seems that Mr. Browne is on a great big roll.

I will resist the temptation to call him Scott, even though I know that's what his mom calls him. His proud mom is my friend Carolyn Vecchio Brown, Vallejo High – Class of 1960. By the way, I was greatly relieved to read the dedication: "For my parents. Thank you for believing." This is much better than *Breathers* where mom and dad wound up as the main course at a barbeque.

Back to *Fated*. Fabio has an important job as it concerns the lives of human beings. He must assign the fate of 83% of the humans born each day, those that will be on the Path of Fate. What about the other 17%? They are on the Path of Destiny, destined to do something special, something great, perhaps something miraculous. Fabio used to take care of his job on a personal level, but the numbers have gotten out of hand. Now he uses a computer program that he runs from his laptop, distributing fates according to a carefully constructed algorithm.

As we get to know Fabio, we learn that the Immortals can put on a man suit or a woman suit and walk among us. We meet the personification of several of his Immortal friends. He has non-contact sex with Destiny, a ravishing redhead. He hangs out with Gluttony and Sloth. He crosses paths with Dennis, the name that Death goes by. He also encounters Karma, that always-interesting blend of fate and destiny who, according to Fabio, tends to hang out in India. All of these colleagues have personalities and they are not always what you'd expect. Fabio reveals their traits through a steady stream of one-liners:

"The thing about Destiny is that she's a nymphomaniac."
Or, "The thing about Karma is that he's an alcoholic."
Or, "The thing about Lady Luck is she has ADD."
And of course, "The thing about Jerry is that he's a control freak."
The plot unfolds masterfully and Browne's wry sense of humor is present on every page. At times the humor is right up front, such as when Fabio recounts an email sent to the entire staff by Jerry. The subject line: "Important!!!" The body of the message: "Big event coming!!! Stay tuned!!!" Fabio tells us:

> This is typical Jerry. He likes to keep us in the dark about his personal projects. Build up suspense. Make a big deal of promoting some big history-changing event and then fill us in on the details at the last moment. Noah. Jesus. The 1969 Mets.

At other times, the humor is much more subtle, at least for me. I had to read this passage several times before it sunk in:

> By the way, the Burning Bush? That was Destiny. She is, after all, a redhead. And fourteen hundred years before the birth of Christ, nobody had ever heard of a Brazilian wax.

Getting back to Rule #1—don't get involved: Fabio absolutely annihilates that one. He falls in love with Sara Griffen, a mortal woman.

She loves him back and they have a wonderful affair. He also begins to alter the fates of some of the humans on his path, trying to improve their lot. Inevitably this gets him in trouble with Jerry. He is called on the carpet and eventually loses his job and his immortality. This all plays out in a wonderful twist of destiny—not fate—but I won't spoil the ending for you.

A reader can take away many lessons from *Fated*. For me it boils down to this: God makes the rules. If we break them there are severe consequences. And, He is not through with His personal projects, those big history-changing events. Stay tuned!

If you don't mind a little gentle irreverence, *Fated* is great fun and I highly recommend it. Browne had me smiling—even laughing out loud—throughout. I think it is safe to say that we are witnessing the beginning of a remarkable career.

A Tale of Three Books

The Paris Wife
Paula McClain
Ballantine Books
2011

A Moveable Feast
Ernest Hemingway
Scribner
1964, edited by Mary Hemingway and Harry Brague

A Moveable Feast, The Restored Edition
Ernest Hemingway
Scribner
2009, edited by Sean Hemingway

The Paris Wife by Paula McClain is a novel about the early years of Ernest Hemingway's career. It covers the years 1921 through 1926, the same period covered in Hemingway's memoir *A Moveable Feast*. I read *Feast* when it was first published in 1964, three years after Hemingway's death, and after finishing *Paris Wife*, it seemed like high time to read it again. In the process, I learned that there is a new release of *A Moveable Feast*, subtitled *The Restored Edition*, edited by Hemingway's grandson Sean. And there is a controversy regarding which version of the book was published as the author intended.

And so we have A Tale of Three Books.

The Paris Wife
Paula McClain's novel tells the story of Hemingway's early struggles to become a writer through the eyes of his first wife, Hadley Richardson. It begins with their courtship in Chicago and St. Louis, and then their marriage and the move to Paris.

In Paris, we see the relationships formed with Gertrude Stein, Ezra Pound, Ford Maddox Ford, Scott and Zelda Fitzgerald, and others of the famed Lost Generation. We see the writer working hard, trying to perfect a new and distinctive style. We live through the devastating loss of his manuscripts—all of his early work—as Hadley is preparing to transport them to him on a train from Paris to Lausanne, Switzerland. We share their joy at the birth of their son John Hadley Nicanor Hemingway, whom they immediately tag with the nickname Bumby. The narrative carries us through the publication of *Three Stories and Ten Poems, In Our Time, The Torrents of Spring*, and up to the point where *The Sun Also Rises* is about to be published. At that time, Hemingway had begun an affair with Pauline Pfeiffer who would eventually become his second wife. What was a story of two people (Hadley and Ernest) deeply in love, poor but very happy, comes to a heartbreaking end.

There is ample evidence of the impact that Hadley had on Hemingway's career. *In Our Time* is dedicated to her. *The Sun Also Rises* is also dedicated to her and to their son John; and Hemingway arranged for the royalties from the book to be paid to her. After divorcing Hemingway, she enjoyed a long and happy marriage to Paul Mowrer, an American journalist.

When I first picked up *The Paris Wife*, my impression was that it read too much like a romance novel. Then the setting moved to Paris and things got very interesting. I kept my dog-eared copy of *The Complete Short Stories of Ernest Hemingway* close at hand, so that I could pick it up to read old favorites as they were mentioned, or alluded to, in the novel: "Up In Michigan," "My Old Man," "A Canary for One," "Summer People." In the end, Paula McClain's novel is a very good read. I finished it several weeks ago and it's still on my mind.

And now for those other two books.

A Moveable Feast – the original publication
The Original version was published in 1964, edited by Mary Hemingway, Ernest's fourth wife and widow, and Harry Brague of Scribners. According to Mary, Hemingway began work on the book in 1957, worked on it in various places through 1959, then set it aside to write *The Dangerous Summer*. He completed the book, then called *Paris Sketches,* at his farm in Cuba in the spring of 1960.

In November of 1959, Hemingway sent a draft of the manuscript to Scribners, hand-carried by his friend A.E. Hotchner from Cuba to New York City. Hotchner would eventually write a wonderful biography of Hemingway's later years titled *Papa Hemingway*. After Hemingway's death, Mary decided that Scribners should move ahead with publication. While the book was still in galleys, Hotchner suggested a title based on a conversation that he recalled from 1950 in which Hemingway said:

> If you are lucky enough to have lived in Paris as a
> young man, then wherever you go for the rest of your
> life, it stays with you, for Paris is a moveable feast.

Hotchner says he read the manuscript on the plane from Cuba to New York, and the version that was originally published is substantially as the author intended. The original includes a preface, in the form of a letter from Hemingway, plus twenty sketches. If you've read the book, I'm sure you have your favorites. Mine are the profiles of Gertrude Stein, Silvia Beach, Ford Madox Ford, Ezra Pound, and of course, Scott and Zelda Fitzgerald. In other chapters, the author paints a vivid picture of Paris: the café scene, the gardens and museums, living in the poorer quarters of the city, the racetracks nearby, and even the weather. If you can read it and not have the urge to book a flight to Paris, you're a stronger person than I am.

A Moveable Feast – The Restored Edition

In 1979, Hemingway's papers, housed at the John F. Kennedy Library in Boston, were opened to the public. Since that time, scholars have questioned Mary Hemingway's edits, pointing out that the order of chapters in the author's final draft had been changed, and that a chapter titled "Birth of a New School," which Hemingway had dropped, was reinserted. In addition, a lengthy apology to Hadley, which was included in every draft, was deleted.

Sean Hemingway, the author's grandson, took up the cause and published *The Restored Edition* in 2009. Patrick Hemingway, the author's sole surviving son, lent his approval to the project and wrote a personal foreword for the book. The foundation for Sean's work is a typed draft with Hemingway's handwritten notations. Sean makes it clear that the book was never finished in Hemingway's eyes. The author made a list of possible titles to replace *Paris Sketches*, and only three of the chapters had been given titles. Hemingway drafted a letter (never mailed) to Charles Scribner, Jr., in April, 1961, saying that the book lacked a proper introduction and a closing chapter. He suggested that it be published "as is," since he felt unable to complete the work.

The new edition supposedly restores the order of the chapters and the final content intended by the author. There are nineteen sketches in the main body of the text. In addition, Sean presents ten sketches that were left out of the final draft by the author, many of which had never been published in any form. He also includes a series of fragments that show Hemingway struggling to capture certain thoughts as his mental health deteriorated.

Controversy and Conclusions

The points of contention between the original and the restored versions of *A Moveable Feast* are numerous and clear.

First, there is the assertion by Mary Hemingway that the author considered the book finished, a contention rebutted by the author's own words. Second, there is the reordering of the chapters and the reinsertion of deleted material. Third, there is the deletion of the "apology" to Hadley which appeared in every draft. Finally, Sean contends that the letter from Hemingway that serves as the preface in the original was fabricated by Mary from several fragments found in the author's papers.

On the other hand, we have A.E. Hotchner's statement that he read Hemingway's draft in 1959 and that the original version was substantially as the author intended. In a scathing article in the *New York Times*, Hotchner accused Sean of altering a masterpiece in order to make his grandmother, Pauline Pfeiffer, look like less of a villain in the breakup of Hemingway's first marriage.

I came into this with the inclination to believe Mr. Hotchner, mainly because I am a big fan of his biography, *Papa Hemingway*, published in 1969. That said, I finally have to fall on the side of Patrick and Sean. The Restored Edition makes a compelling case, and several of the chapters are clearly more complete and final.

For example, the chapter titled "Winters in Schruns" is a stunningly beautiful description of alpine skiing in the Austrian Vorarlberg. In the original, this chapter was mashed-up with the material that now appears as "The Pilot Fish and the Rich," one of the Additional Sketches that Sean says the author intended to omit.

"The Pilot Fish" chapter includes the material that reads as an indictment of Pauline Pfeiffer. It includes Hemingway's description of being in love with two women and his apology to Hadley. In one incredibly moving paragraph, he describes returning to his family in Austria after a trip to New York to negotiate with his publisher:

> When I saw my wife again standing by the tracks as the train came in by the piled logs at the station, I wished I had died before I ever loved anyone but her. She was smiling, the sun on her lovely face tanned by the snow and sun, beautifully built, her hair red gold in the sun, grown out all winter awkwardly and beautifully, and Mr. Bumby standing with her, blond and chunky and with winter cheeks looking like a good Vorarlberg boy.

As I said, I have to side with *The Restored Edition*, and I'm grateful to Sean Hemingway, whatever his motives, for presented the previously unpublished sketches and fragments.

Remembering what the author was going through in early 1961, struggling with depression and mental illness, having received electric shock treatments at the Mayo Clinic in Rochester, Minnesota, I agree with Patrick Hemingway that the following fragment is the true foreword to *A Moveable Feast*:

> This book contains material from the *remises* of my memory and of my heart. Even if the one has been tampered with and the other does not exist.

And there you have it: a tale of three books. One a fine novel, the other two competing editions of a classic memoir. As with all things Hemingway, damn fine reads.

Remembering Mr. Lincoln

Team of Rivals –
The Political Genius of Abraham Lincoln
Doris Kearns Goodwin
Simon & Schuster, 2005

This is not a movie review, but it definitely began with a movie. I saw *Lincoln* about two months ago and noticed this in the credits: "Based on *Team of Rivals*, by Doris Kearns Goodwin." I loved the movie and immediately had the urge to know more, the urge to read the book. At nine hundred and sixteen pages, including one hundred and twenty-one pages of notes, it had to be a strong urge.

Political Genius
Doris Kearns Goodwin has provided a remarkable piece of work, thoroughly researched and documented, written in clean, clear-cut prose. She won the Pulitzer Prize for this book, and it seems well-deserved. Over the course of all those pages, backed up by her copious notes and references, she proves the point of her sub-title: Lincoln was indeed a political genius.

The evidence is documented in the way in which Lincoln won the Republican Party's nomination for president in 1860. He campaigned skillfully to hold the first ballot "favorite son" vote from the Illinois delegation, and then positioned himself to be the logical "second choice" if the front-runners faltered, which they ultimately did.

Lincoln's genius was also evidenced in the way, time and time again, he turned his bitterest rivals into allies, and even staunch supporters. William Henry Seward, Salmon P. Chase, and Edward Bates were all considered strong candidates for the Republican nomination in 1860. All of them had stronger credentials than Lincoln. Yet when Lincoln was nominated and won the election, he brought all three into his cabinet where they served with distinction. William Stanton had deliberately snubbed Lincoln in the course of a major lawsuit. Yet

Lincoln recognized his managerial talent and made him Secretary of War. Stanton served with great distinction in that post and deserves much credit for the success of the Union cause.

Another point of Lincoln's genius was his political timing. He seemed to have the pulse of the people in knowing just when to issue an executive order or proclamation. The Emancipation Proclamation is a prime example. The political factions in the northern states were deeply divided over the question of slavery, and even those who wanted to see the institution die were not willing to "...fight a war for the black man." Lincoln picked the perfect time to issue the Emancipation Proclamation, and to begin enlisting blacks into the army. In the end, over one hundred and eighty thousand black men served on the Union side, arguably turning the tide in the war.

Unforgettable Images
The book is full of unforgettable facts and images, things we may have learned in history classes but have long forgotten.

First and foremost, there is the fact that more than six hundred thousand Americans (North and South) died in the Civil War. Goodwin points out that this is more than all the nation's wars since that time *combined*. Think about that for a minute: World Wars I and II, Korea, Vietnam, Iraq, Afghanistan, not to mention the lesser conflicts that dot our history.

In the first major battle of the Civil War, at Antietam (the first Battle of Bull Run), it is amazing how close the Union came to having Washington D.C. captured by Confederate troops. Soundly defeated in battle, The Army of the Potomac came streaming back into Washington in total disarray. If the rebels had not stopped to regroup, the Capitol could have been overrun. It is quite likely, then, that Britain, France, and Spain would have formally recognized the Confederacy and lent support to their cause. The Union side came that close to losing the war.

Another striking point was how freely President Lincoln moved about a war-torn country. He made a dozen trips in four years to the front lines, traveling by boat, carriage, and horseback. He walked the streets of Richmond, the Confederate capital, the day after the city was taken by the Union army. Think of the modern day equivalents: Truman walking the streets of Berlin or Tokyo; G.W. Bush in Baghdad. These situations are unimaginable today.

Goodwin emphasizes Lincoln's belief in the absolute necessity of preserving the union. This belief was firmly rooted in the Declaration of Independence and the Constitution, to which Lincoln would return again and again. The Gettysburg Address is the classic summary of Lincoln's unshakable belief, set to words most of us have had to memorize at one time or another. He clearly saw our experiment in "...government of the people, by the people, for the people" as a cause worth defending at all costs.

Finally, Goodwin makes it clear that there were many remarkable women who influenced history during the Civil War Era. Mary Todd Lincoln, Kate Chase, and Frances Seward could all be subjects of compelling books and movies. Frances Seward in particular presents as an articulate and passionate spokeswoman for the cause of abolition.

The Book and the Movie
It is a major stretch for *Lincoln* the movie to proclaim "...based on *Team of Rivals*." The portion of the book devoted to the passage of the Thirteenth Amendment—the central conflict in the movie—is a couple of pages at most. Thaddeus Stevens, the role that Tommy Lee Jones plays so brilliantly in the movie, barely rates a mention in the book.

Tony Kushner's screenplay is, in reality, an original work—with a few Doris Kearns Goodwin quotes thrown in for good measure. And, Mr. Kushner and Mr. Spielberg should have read the ending of book more closely: it is much more dramatic than the movie.

Conclusion
If you are a lover of history, then I highly recommend *Team of Rivals*. Goodwin brings the historical characters to life, warts and all. As I said earlier, there is enough prime material here for several movies. And if one of your New Year's resolutions is to get more exercise, just carrying the book around for several weeks will provide a great workout. Enjoy!

John Henry Holliday

Doc
Mary Doria Russell
Ballantine Books, 2011

Doc is the story of the life and times of John Henry "Doc" Holliday, up to and including his time in Dodge City, Kansas, but prior to Tombstone, Arizona, and the gunfight at the O.K. Corral. This vein has been mined so many times, you'd think there would be little new to say. And yet Russell gives us a fresh take on events in the famous cow town by focusing on Doc Holliday rather than Wyatt Earp and his brothers.

The Doc Holliday presented here is well-educated, a graduate of a respected dental college in Philadelphia, a lover of music and literature, and a gentleman of impeccable manners who spoke with a lovely, melodic Georgia drawl. At twenty-one, he was diagnosed with tuberculosis. He left his home and family in Georgia and headed west where the climate was supposed to be better for his health. After a time in Texas, where he hooked-up with the prostitute "Big Nose" Kate Harony, he headed for Dodge City, arriving in 1878 at the age of twenty-six.

Russell does a fine job of developing all the characters Doc meets in Dodge City, including the Earp brothers (Morgan, Wyatt, and James), a Jesuit priest Fr. Alexander von Angensperg, John Horse Sanders, and Jau "China Joe" Dong-Sing, among many others. These are complex people living in a challenging time and place. There are no saints here; everyone has mixed motives and agendas, including our hero.

Perhaps the most vivid portrait Russell paints is that of Big Nose Kate Harony. She was born in Hungary to a family of would-be aristocrats. The story of how the family was devastated by events and Kate was left destitute and alone is a fascinating tale in itself. She would be Doc Holliday's woman, off and on, through the last nine years of his life.

As I said, this material has been covered again and again, especially in movies and television. Which raises an interesting question: who was your favorite in the role of Doc Holliday? Here is a brief recap of the actors who have played the Deadly Dentist.

Victor Mature in *My Darling Clementine*, 1946. Directed by John Ford. Henry Fonda as Wyatt Earp.

Douglas Fowley and **Myron Healy** in *The Life and Legend of Wyatt Earp*, 1955 – 1961, ABC TV. Fowley appeared in forty-six episodes. Myron Healy played Doc in ten episodes. Hugh O'Brien played Wyatt.

Kirk Douglas in *Gunfight at the O.K. Corral*, 1957. Directed by John Sturges. Burt Lancaster as Wyatt.

Jason Robards in *Hour of the Gun*, 1967. Directed again by John Sturges, this version supposedly closer to the factual events. James Garner as Wyatt.

Val Kilmer in *Tombstone*, 1993. A troubled project that eventually had two directors: George Pan Cosmatos, followed by Kevin Jarre. Kurt Russell as Wyatt.

Dennis Quaid in *Wyatt Earp*, 1994. Directed by Lawrence Kasdan. Kevin Costner as Wyatt.

Most of us baby boomers became aware of the Earp/Holliday legend from the TV show, beginning in the mid-fifties. I can't say that I remember much about Douglas Fowley or Myron Healy's portrayal, probably because they only appeared in a quarter of the two hundred and twenty-nine episodes.

Victor Mature was charming in *My Darling Clementine* and Kirk Douglas was intense (picture Spartacus in a cowboy hat) in *Gunfight*, but both of them were too robust and healthy looking.

Hour of the Gun was a forgettable film and Jason Robards was just too old to play a man who was barely thirty.

Dennis Quaid appears to have starved himself to prepare for the role in *Wyatt Earp*, but like Kirk Douglas, he's all intensity and no charm.

That leaves us with Val Kilmer in *Tombstone*. He looks the part of a young man dying of tuberculosis: frail, wasted, coughing, sweating profusely. And, he speaks with a Southern drawl as smooth and sweet as honey drizzled on a Georgia peach. To top things off, the screenwriter gives him that signature line to recite: "I'm your Huckleberry." Mr. Kilmer takes the crown as the all-time best Doc Holiday.

What's that? You sayin' I'm wrong? I'm countin' to three and you better reach for that hogleg, mister.

Getting back to Mary Doria Russell's novel, *Doc* is a good read and I highly recommend it. The subject matter may be old, but Russell's view is refreshing.

On The Road

The book and the movie...

I got my driver's license in September 1958, about a month before my father passed away. My mom, being the sweet and gullible person that she was, gave me near-complete freedom to use the family car and come and go as I pleased. A few years earlier, the interstate highway engineers had completed The Big Cut, blasting a gap through the hills on the Crockett side of the Carquinez Strait that sent I-80 zooming toward San Francisco in a relatively straight line. No longer did it take an hour to drive to S.F., winding through all the towns along the rim of the bay. Now you could zip from Vallejo to the Bay Bridge in about thirty minutes. And zip we did, many times, to hang out with the Beatniks in North Beach.

Radiating from Upper Grant Avenue, north of Broadway, were the shops and clubs and coffee houses frequented by the Beat Generation. North Beach was to the Beats what Haight-Ashbury became for the Hippies. We'd walk along the streets of the neighborhood, rubbing shoulders with all the colorful characters, listening to the music pouring out of the jazz clubs, peering in the windows of the coffeehouses where poetry was being shouted into open mics.

Years later, I read an article in the *San Francisco Chronicle* that described the night Allen Ginsberg read his poem "Howl" in public. His friend Jack Kerouac went to a local market and bought jugs of cheap red wine and paper cups and then bustled through the coffeehouse crowd keeping everyone's cup full while Ginsberg read.

Did that really happen? I've only seen that one account, but true or false, it was enough—some forty years ago—to motivate me to read Kerouac's *On The Road*, the novel that gave the Beat Generation its name. I loved the book way back then, and so when the movie adaptation was released, I had to see it. And, as usually happens, the movie motivated me to read the novel again.

The Book

On The Road immortalizes the friendship and adventures of Sal Paradise (Kerouac) and Dean Moriarty (Neal Cassady in real life). Among their friends and lovers are Carlo Marx (Allen Ginsberg), Marylou (Dean's sixteen-year-old bride), Camille (Dean's second wife) and Old Bull Lee (the writer William S. Burroughs). There are many other friends that come into the orbit of Sal and Dean, but it is their friendship that drives the story. The plot is pretty simple and is summed up by the title. It's all about being on the road, raging across the country from New York to Denver to San Francisco and back, again and again; sometimes by car, sometimes by bus, but also hitchhiking. Of course there is a trip south to Algiers, Louisiana, to visit Bull Lee, and finally an epic trip into Mexico.

Dean is the energy source for most of these journeys, bouncing from one wife to the next and back again, and forever in search of his father, Dean, Sr., who is a bum believed to be living on the streets of various cities, depending on the season. Dean is the bad boy that Sal hangs out with and hangs on to, knowing full well that he is an amoral con man and will ultimately break the hearts of all the people who love him.

After forty years, Kerouac's prose still fascinates me: the passionate, highly-charged sentences that go on forever, words strung together randomly, yet making perfect sense in the end. There are passages I never forgot from my first reading, and I smiled when I came to them again. Here is a sample in which Sal learns that Dean is on his way to Denver from New York, intending to be the driver on their adventure to Mexico:

> Suddenly I had a vision of Dean, a burning shuddering frightful Angel, palpitating toward me across the road, pursuing me like the Shrouded Traveler on the plain, bearing down on me. I saw his huge face over the plains with the mad, bony purpose and the gleaming eyes; I saw his wings; I saw the old jalopy chariot with thousands of sparking flames shooting out from it; I saw the path it burned over the road; it even made its own road and went over the corn, through cities, destroying bridges, drying rivers. It came like wrath to the West...

A brief aside: in 2009, when my friend Bruce Bigelow came driving west from New Mexico to attend the fifty-year reunion of the Vallejo High School Class of 1959, I conjured up the passage above and saw Bruce's jet black Corvette bearing down on my home in Carmichael, flames shooting from the tailpipes. Funny how words on a page stick in your mind.

I will admit that the narrative got a little tedious when I was about two thirds of the way through the book. But then the Mexico trip grabbed my attention and propelled me through to the end. When I read the final emotion-packed paragraph, I was both happy and sad: happy that I took the time to read *On The Road* again; sad that it was over.

The Movie

I think the producers had low expectations, given that the movie went to On Demand the same day it opened in theaters. You'll have a hard time finding it at your local multiplex; it came and went very quickly.

Kristen Stewart (Marylou) got a lot of attention for her nude scenes, though her role was rather limited. Viggo Mortensen earned glowing reviews for his supporting role as Old Bull Lee, though Amy Adams is wasted in the role of Lee's wife Jane. Kirsten Dunst is quite good as Camille and Sam Riley is a very credible Sal.

For me, the actor who carries the film is Garrett Hedlund as Dean. His performance is award-worthy. He is not quite the mad prophet and deranged instigator of adventure that Kerouac paints in the novel, but he is damn close. He becomes that bad boy you can't help but love, no matter what he does.

And now we get to my pet peeve: filmmakers who have the unmitigated *chutzpah* to rewrite a classic piece of literature. Walter Salles is the director; the screenwriter is Jose Rivera. It seems that together they have invented things that are not in the original work. For example, the open homo- and bisexuality. It isn't in the book, and yet it is presented graphically in the film.

Then there is the relationship between Sal and Marylou, the beautiful girl that Dean married so young. Even though at one point, Dean attempts to give her to Sal, in the book Marylou and Sal never consummate the union. Yet in the film, the two of them have vigorous, straight-ahead sex, a scene in which Kristen Stewart is outstanding (no pun intended).

In defense of Salles and Rivera, I've read that they depended less on the published book and more on Kerouac's original manuscript, which was typed on a continuous one hundred and twenty foot roll of teletype paper with all the real names left in.

There is far more material in the novel than could be included in the film and some tough choices had to be made. For instance, Sal meets a beautiful Mexican girl, Teresa, on a Greyhound Bus. They start out sitting across the aisle, then together, then making out and pledging their undying love. They wander from L.A. to her hometown in the Central Valley, living in a tent city and picking cotton in the fields. She has a young son and Sal seems willing to assume the role of stepfather. At the end of the cotton season, Sal leaves to return to New York with the understanding that Teresa will follow him soon. He knows, even as he's leaving, that he'll never see her again. It is a very touching segment of the book and it's too bad it didn't make the cut.

In spite of the filmmakers' *futsing* with a classic, the movie does a good job of capturing the spirit of *On The Road*. I'm glad that I took the time to watch it, and I think you will like it too—if you can find it.

Book in Search of a Movie

The Art of Fielding
Chad Harbach
Little, Brown and Company
First edition, 2011

The Art of Fielding is Chad Harbach's first novel and it is generating a lot of buzz following a strong review in the New York Times, not to mention great word of mouth. The notes on the dustcover summarize the plot perfectly:

> At Westish College, a small school on the shore of Lake Michigan, baseball star Henry Skrimshander seems destined for big-league stardom. But when a routine throw goes disastrously off course, the fates of five people are upended.
>
> Henry's fight against self-doubt threatens to ruin his future. College president Guert Affenlight, a longtime bachelor, has fallen unexpectedly and helplessly in love. Owen Dunne, Henry's gay roommate and teammate, becomes caught up in a dangerous affair. Mike Schwartz, the team captain and Henry's best friend, realizes he has guided Henry's career at the expense of his own. And Pella Affenlight, Guert's daughter, returns to Westish after escaping an ill-fated marriage, determined to start a new life.

Yes, *The Art of Fielding* is about baseball. But it is so much more. It is really about relationships: the ups and downs, twists and turns, that all of these deeply flawed characters experience. At the heart of the story are Henry and Mike. And then Guert and Pella, Guert and Owen, Pella and Mike, Pella and Henry, and on it goes.

The Westish Harpooners are in the midst of an historic season, bound for a conference title and a berth in the national tournament. Westish has never won a conference title, and seldom experienced a winning season. At the heart of this turnaround are Henry and Mike. Henry is driven, since his days in Little League, to be the perfect shortstop. This quest has become his life and he is on the verge of breaking a collegiate record for consecutive errorless games. Mike has pushed Henry toward perfection, not only honing his fielding skills, but packing on pounds of lean muscle and turning Henry into a fearsome clutch hitter.

On the eve of his triumphant achievement, with major league scouts crowding the stands at every game, suddenly Henry contracts Steve Blass Disease. Steve Blass was a fine pitcher who led the Pittsburgh Pirates to a World Series title in 1971. At spring training in 1973, suddenly Blass could not throw a strike. Two years later, he retired. Other players have been infected over the years: Mackey Sasser, a catcher who could not hit the pitcher from sixty feet away; Steve Sax and Chuck Knoblauch, second basemen who could no longer make the throw to first; Rick Ankiel, a pitcher who, like Blass, could no longer throw a strike. Only Sax ever really recovered. Knoblauch and Ankiel had to move to the outfield where the throws are less precise.

Harbach provides an intense and detailed description of what Henry is going through, as in the following passage:

> ...Henry knew where the ball was headed before the swing was half finished, a sharp grounder three steps to his left, ideal for a double play. He was there waiting when the ball arrived. Ajay darted over to cover second. Henry, still low in his crouch, pivoted and whipped his arm sidelong across his body, just as he'd practiced so many thousands of times, but at the last moment he sensed the throw would be too hard for Ajay to handle, so he tried to decelerate slightly, but no, that was wrong too. But it was too late, the ball left his hand and began sliding rightward, out into the path of the charging runner, and Ajay, all five-foot-five of him, tried to stretch to make the catch, but the ball caught the tip of his glove and scooted into short right field ...

If you are a former ballplayer, this is agonizing stuff to read, because chances are, you've been there and you'd rather not think about it. You find yourself pulling—even praying— for Henry to snap out of it, knowing full well from your own experience that it isn't likely to happen.

All of Harbach's characters are affected by Henry's struggles, especially Mike, Pella, Guert, and Owen. Nobody comes out unscathed. Much like the movie version of Bernard Malamud's "The Natural," you have to suspend disbelief to accept Harbach's resolution of the myriad issues. And, he takes some aspects of the plot in directions that I didn't like.

That said, this is a terrific novel, one that is a must read, especially if you have ever played the game of baseball. You former players will know the Westish Harpooners, only by different names, and you'll smile at all the familiar idiosyncrasies that Harbach depicts so accurately.

In the final chapter, you will also see a brilliant opening for a sequel. Hey, if John Updike could do it, why not Chad Harbach? In the meantime, we can all amuse ourselves by casting the characters for the movie version. How about Richard Gere for Guert Affenlight? Emma Stone for Pella? Ron Shelton to write the screenplay and direct? I could go on; we'll compare notes later.

Wild

The Book and the Movie

From the moment I saw the cover of *Wild: From Lost to Found on the Pacific Crest Trail,* I couldn't wait to read the book. That picture of the battered hiking boot rang bells and pushed all my buttons. The book was published in 2012, but back in 2002, my son Matt and I took a backpacking trip on the Pacific Crest Trail (PCT), and even though it was a short four-day hike, it was a memorable experience.

And so I bought the book and read eagerly, waiting for the time when the author, Cheryl Strayed, would reach the part of the trail—Barker Pass to Echo Lake—that we had hiked. As it turns out, in the year that she hiked the PCT, the High Sierra was socked in under heavy snow well into the summer. She had to bypass that portion of the trail.

That was my only disappointment in reading the book. I loved it! And so I rushed out to see the movie when it was released.

Herewith, my thoughts on the book and the movie.

The Book

In 1995, four years after her mother died of cancer at the age of forty-five, the author found her life spiraling into a black hole. She had destroyed her marriage to a man she still loved, found herself engaging in casual sex with numerous men, had an affair with a man who introduced her to heroin, wound up pregnant and decided to have an abortion. Her brother, sister, and step-father had all drifted away into separate lives, her once close-knit family dissolved.

In the midst of all this turmoil, she saw a copy of *The Pacific Crest Trail, Volume 1: California* on a book rack in an REI store. An idea began to form in her mind. Later she would return and buy the book, and from there grew the plan to hike the PCT from Mojave, California, near its southern end, to Ashland, Oregon. With the subsequent bypass of the High Sierra, she extended her goal to The Bridge of the Gods on the Columbia River, the border between Oregon and Washington.

By taking herself completely out of the life she was living, maybe—just maybe—she could find the woman she was supposed to be. She walked more than 1,100 miles, alone, from June until mid-September. When she reached The Bridge of the Gods, you knew she had made it, physically and emotionally.

The years that followed proved this to be true. Cheryl is married, the mother of two, and an author who will see her future works gobbled up by a large group of admirers, myself among them.

I enjoyed the book more the second time around. I could feel the weight of her pack on my shoulders, the waist belt biting into my hips, and the sickening realization that it is far heavier than it should be. Her descriptions of the trail, the obstacles she encounters and the people she meets, all seemed familiar. But there are multiple narratives taking place as she struggles northward. In each chapter, she provides a glimpse into her life, reaching back to her childhood with an abusive, alcoholic father, moving on through the devastating loss of her mother, and into the self-destructive life that nearly consumed her after her mother's death.

Cheryl Strayed is a damn fine writer. Her prose is clear and concise. *Wild* is a confessional and she appears to have held nothing back. She is brutally honest about her failures and it is easy to get pissed-off at her. How could she be so stupid, so self-destructive? But all of *that* is what drove her to the PCT. Eleven hundred miles later, you know she has achieved her goal and you have to admire the accomplishment.

The Movie

My son-in-law, David Grazer, likes to remind me that when Hollywood buys the rights to a book, they are buying the title, and maybe the general idea. From there, all bets are off. The screenplay and the resulting movie are an adaptation; they may or may not be true to the original work. He is absolutely right.

That said, *Wild* the movie is an award-worthy adaptation. Directed by Jean-Marc Vallee with a screenplay by Nick Hornby, it adopts the same structure as the book. There is the monumental struggle of the trail, and then there are the flashbacks to Cheryl's life story, and the creative team manages to hit nearly all the highlights. In any adaptation, hard choices have to be made, unless you want to end up with a four-hour film. Of course, they change a little here and add a little there, but all things considered, the spirit of the book comes through intact.

The author makes a cameo appearance at the beginning of the film—she is driving the truck that drops Cheryl off in Mojave—so I took that as a stamp of approval for what follows.

Reese Witherspoon is terrific as Cheryl, underplaying effectively at times, but giving full release to her emotions when it's called for. Laura Dern gives an amazing performance as Bobbi, Cheryl's mother. She holds nothing back and dominates nearly every scene she is in. I'll be pulling for both of them on Oscar night.

Here is my recommendation: read the book, then go out and see the movie, and then root for Reese, Laura Dern, and Nick Hornby all through the awards season. I guarantee that when Cheryl arrives at the Bridge of the Gods—in the book and in the movie—you will have tears in your eyes, if not on your cheeks.

Wild is that good.

Appalachian Gray

Gray Mountain
John Grisham
Doubleday, 2014

Gray Mountain is the story of Samantha Kofer, a young associate with a giant Wall Street law firm, working in the real estate division. Her job primarily involves the review and drafting of contracts. She has never seen the inside of a courtroom. The financial crisis of 2008 begins to sweep through the economy and firms up and down The Street are downsizing. Samantha's firm closes down the real estate practice and she, along with several hundred other associates, are "furloughed." The firm's furlough agreement provides that she can keep her health care benefits if she finds a position—somewhere, anywhere—as an unpaid legal intern. She finds an internship with a legal aid clinic in rural Appalachia, in the fictional town of Brady, Virginia, the heart of coal country. In very short order, she is immersed in cases involving real people with real problems and no means of paying for legal representation. She even finds herself in court on a regular basis.

The people Samantha meets and the problems they face drive Grisham's story. It doesn't take her long to realize that there are significant rewards in helping people in need, rewards that extend beyond the Wall Street salary and the excitement of being young and single in Manhattan. She also meets an attorney in Brady who has a tragic family history and has made it his life's work to take on the coal companies, battling them through the legal system over their abuse of the environment, the mine workers, and the people of Appalachia generally.

The picture Grisham paints of Big Coal and its practices in the Appalachian region is shocking, to say the least. They rape the environment through the practice of mountaintop-removal mining, a form of strip mining that involves decapitating a mountain to get to the seams of coal deep below the surface. The upper layers, termed "overburden," are bulldozed into the surrounding valleys, destroying the habitat and clogging the natural streams. The laws authorizing this form of mining require the companies to restore the habitat once the coal has been extracted, but it seems this is seldom accomplished.

If you want to see what mountaintop-removal mining looks like, click on the following link http://www.plunderingappalachia.org/ and watch the video. This is the fate of about five hundred mountains in Appalachia, so far. "Clean coal technology," a phrase politicians love to use, may be the ultimate oxymoron.

The coal companies treat the miners as brutally as they treat the environment. Black lung disease is common among the mine workers, but if a miner files a claim for compensation from a fund set up for this purpose, the companies contest the claim regardless of the facts. The average time to resolve a claim is five to seven years. The companies know they spend more fighting an individual claim that it would take to pay the awarded benefits. They contest the claims simply to intimidate the miners and discourage them from filing in the first place.

In the Oscar-winning movie *Unforgiven*, Little Bill Daggett (Gene Hackman) is lying on the floor of a saloon mortally wounded; he looks up and says, "I don't deserve this … to die like this…" William Munny (Clint Eastwood)—aiming a rifle at Little Bill's head—says, "Deserve's got nothing to do with it." The people of Appalachia deserve better, and they certainly do not deserve to die like this. But, I'm afraid deserve has nothing to do with it.

As the story progresses, Samantha wins some and loses some for her clients, and she struggles to decide whether or not to return to New York and her city girl lifestyle. But the major arc of the story revolves around a law suit filed against one of the coal companies and its lawyers, and the lengths they will go to in order to quash the suit. Like most Grisham tales, it is a legal adventure thriller and he keeps you turning the pages, anxious to find out what will happen next.

Gray Mountain is a good read and well worth your attention. When you finally put it down, pick up your pen and write to your congressperson, your senators, and the White House. Appalachia should not be a third-world country ruled by Big Coal. The people really do deserve better.

IV.

Monterey Diary

Where were you in September of 2000?

Tuesday, September 12, 2000

Two more days to go. I can't believe it is almost here: The Forty-third Annual Monterey Jazz Festival. I remember how excited I was in 1958, the festival's first year. It was the only great West Coast festival and I knew that Monterey was accessible for a kid living in Northern California. Someday I would be there, listening to the greatest artists in jazz. And I did get there, several times, for an individual show or two, but never for the entire festival. This year will be a first. All three nights and two days. Total immersion.

Friday morning, I'll pack the car and hit the road around 10:30 a.m. or so. I waited too long to book a room, but I was able to get a campsite reservation at Sunset Beach State Park. I can check in at the park after 2:00 p.m. That will give me plenty of time to set up camp, relax for a while, and then head to the Monterey Fairgrounds for the Friday night show. I couldn't get tickets to the main arena, but it doesn't matter. The Friday and Saturday performers play the other venues around the grounds as well as the main stage. And the main stage shows are simulcast to a theater. It's all good.

All I have to do now is get through Wednesday and Thursday. I've never been good at waiting patiently.

Friday, September 15, 2000

Barbara wakes me at 5:30 a.m. as she is leaving for Los Angeles. She is on her way to deliver my son Matt's new car, the car he doesn't know is coming. It should be a great surprise. For a moment, I'm more excited about Matt's reaction than I am about the festival.

I can't get back to sleep, so I finally crawl out of bed. Usually, with some place fun to go, I'm up and running, but I can't seem to get going. I knock around, make some coffee, read the newspaper, and then I force myself to make a list of things to do before I can leave. That gets me started.

Sammi, our adopted cat, scoots in and out of the house and the garage while I am packing the car. She knows something is going on. At last the car is packed. I fill Sammi's water bottle with fresh water, give her a scratch on the head, and hit the road around 11:30.

———

It's about 3:00 p.m. when I arrive at Sunset Beach. The weather is Chamber of Commerce gorgeous, sunny and bright and clear. I pick a campsite in a grove of Monterey Pines, just across from the rest rooms and showers, as is the Spooner tradition. I set up my twenty-dollar Sears Roebuck two-man tent and start to inflate the air mattress. Just then a squirrel scurries into my camp and comes directly to me, completely unafraid. He stands on his hind legs like he's begging for a treat. Then he starts to climb up my leg. I wouldn't mind if I was wearing long pants, but standing there in shorts those little paws feel pretty weird. I shoo him off and he eventually leaves in search of friendlier campers.

To the east of the campground, behind the showers, is a rolling field completely covered in plastic in preparation for the planting of strawberries. To the north is a long row of greenhouses. This is obviously a major strawberry operation.

The drive in from Highway 1, heading west toward the beach, winds through miles of fields planted in strawberries, cabbage, lettuce, and other row crops. Along the way, you see crews of a dozen or so men stooped over the rows, working across the fields. At the edge of the fields, you see battered cars and buses and behind the buses are trailers mounted with portable toilets. A hundred years of automation and still the only way to tend these crops is by stoop labor. It is a scene from *The Grapes of Wrath.*

———

Around 5:30 p.m., I head out of the campground for Monterey. On the way, I spot a set of stairs climbing the giant sand dunes that separate the camping area from the beach. I park and climb the stairs to take a look. The stairway ends at an observation platform. From there you can see the whole sweep of Monterey Bay, from Pacific Grove to Santa Cruz. I make a note to come back at night if it is clear and see the lights all around the bay.

And so it's off to Monterey and Fisherman's Wharf for dinner. There's no way I'm going to miss an opportunity to go to the Wharfside Restaurant for their delicious handmade ravioli!

The view of the wharf and the harbor from the second floor of the Wharfside is the same as ever. There are the sport fishing businesses, the party boats docked for the night, and the traditional sea lion swimming around, begging the tourists to toss an anchovy.

The wharf is quiet, very few people on this Friday in mid-September. How many times did I sit here with sons Matt and Gabe, our mouths watering in anticipation of the ravioli? It must have been ten straight summer vacations at least. We'd come here for lunch while Barb, Rachel, and Rachel's friend Christina would shop in Carmel and have lunch at Katy's Cottage. Then we'd meet later at Wisehart's Bakery for a chocolate-striped pretzel and coffee. The ravioli arrives and turns out to be as delicious and changeless as the view.

———

When I arrive at the festival around 7:00 p.m., the fairgrounds are decked out and ready. All the booths are set up and the merchants are at work. A good crowd is on hand early, browsing, eating, and meeting friends from years past. From the west end of the grounds, you hit the food booths first—gumbo, jambalaya, red beans and rice, sweet potato and pecan pie. Large barbeque grills are everywhere, with ribs, chicken, beef, and catfish on the coals, getting ready for the crowds. Someone could drop you here and say you were in New Orleans and you could almost believe it. But the Monterey Pines and the Pacific weather would be a giveaway.

Closer to the main arena, you come to the merchandise booths—art, clothing, hats, tapes, and CDs. There is a booth manned by the Tuskegee Airmen, and a booth selling paraphernalia of the Negro Major Leagues. It strikes me that the whole merchandise section is a celebration of black pride.

It is hard to write anything about this festival without mentioning race. Jazz is an art form invented by black people and its great stars over the years have been black. That is not to say there are no great white jazz musicians. Quite the contrary; jazz became an international art form that draws great musicians from around the world.

Thank God the inventors were so generous as to share this music and allow the world to participate. So if I mention race, it is out of respect and admiration. I know from past visits that the Monterey crowd is a living, breathing rainbow. I'm happy to be a part of it.

I scope out the venues around the fairgrounds. There is the Garden Stage which is a large outdoor amphitheater. There is Dizzy's Den (named in honor of Dizzy Gillespie), The Night Club, and the Jazz Theater, which are all large county fair exhibit halls in real life. And there is the Coffee House Gallery, a smaller space for the more esoteric groups.

I'm zeroed in on Dizzy's Den for the evening. Guitarist Bill Frisell will lead off the program, followed by Richard Bona, and then Diane Reeves. I notice a long line forming for The Den, so I queue up at about 7:40. The doors finally open at 8:00 and we all stream in. Then it's time to wait again for the show to start at 8:30. I find that having "grounds pass" tickets means doing a lot of waiting. By the end of the weekend, my waiting skills will be well developed.

———

Bill Frisell and his quintet open their set and it doesn't take me long to figure out that it's not my cup of tea. I would call his style "cowboy jazz." There is a strong country-western flavor. But he has some hard-driving, crescendo-building moments and the audience responds warmly.

Richard Bona is next up. He is from Cameroon, and though he speaks English, he sings in his native language of Douala. His players are from Cameroon, Seattle, New Jersey, Texas, and Tel Aviv. Richard is warm and funny in his comments between numbers and he is a very engaging performer. He captures the crowd immediately. The music is a wonderful combination of African, Caribbean, and Latin techno-funk. We can't understand a word Richard is singing, but we love him anyway. I sit next to a group of four black ladies and by the end of the set, they are ready to adopt Richard and take him home.

The final act of the evening is vocalist Diane Reeves. It takes a long time for her band to set up, there is so much electronic gear to hook up and tune. She finally comes on at midnight, about a half hour late, and the audience is tired and a little testy. But Diane is wonderful. What a voice and what a range! She blows me away. There is a strong feminist bent to her song selection. She sings:

> *I am an endangered species*
> *I sing no victim's song*
> *I am a woman, I am an artist*
> *And I know where my voice belongs*

Many people leave early, between numbers, and I can't believe they are walking out on this girl. At the end, around 1:15 a.m., she has us all on our feet, whistling and cheering at the top of our collective voice. What a singer! I must add her to my collection.

I notice something about the festival crowd tonight. They love everybody! Even performers we don't completely understand are given warm receptions. It's like the crowd is saying, "Hey, thanks for being here. We're having a great time, we're in a festive mood, and it's just great that you came to perform for us." It will be interesting to see if this holds true throughout the weekend.

———

I arrive back at camp after 2:00 a.m. and I quickly discover that my two-man tent is designed for guys no taller than five feet five inches and less than one hundred and thirty-five pounds. Once in my sleeping bag with the tent door zipped up, I can't straighten my legs. No matter. I'm too tired and happy to care.

Saturday, September 16, 2000

A siren sounds on the strawberry farm, calling the workers to the fields. Even on Saturday morning the crops need to be tended. Out across the fields, a voice hollers, "Viva Mexico!" From far on the other side, two voices respond, "Viva Mexico!" I climb out of the tent just as the sun is coming up. It is 7:00 a.m. and the campground is beginning to stir. I get a campfire started and begin to think about breakfast. I could go into Moss Landing and find a café for some eggs and hash browns, but I've got plenty of food right here. Breakfast will consist of:

> Granola Bars (peanut butter)
> Fruit (plum and nectarine)
> S'Mores

Yes, that's right: S'Mores. Hey, it was too late when I got back to camp last night and I am Jones'ing for my S'Mores. I'm a little embarrassed because my table is out in the open, in plain view of my neighbors. I weigh my hunger for the taste of a well-made S'Mores against the derision of my fellow campers. S'Mores win, hands down. Then fate intervenes: the fire dies out and I have no kindling to get it going again.

After fruit and granola bars, I walk through the camp heading for the path over the sand dunes to the beach. It is a good climb up the side of the dunes, then way, way down to the beach. I can see that coming back is going to be a serious effort, probably with a couple of rest stops.

Once again it is a beautiful day. The fog bank is hanging well out on the bay. The beach stretches north and south as far as you can see. I head south along the water line toward Moss Landing. After about three quarters of a mile, I pass a fisherman casting into the surf. I nod to him and he returns my nod. I stop and turn, thinking to head back to camp, but the fisherman walks toward me to say hello.

He is about my age, maybe a little older, and he looks to be of Japanese or Philippine decent. When he speaks, I recognize a Hawaiian accent. Sure enough, he is from the islands. He served in the Army and did a couple of stints at Ft. Ord. He was also stationed in Germany and he tells me all about camping in Europe. We talk about fishing, the weather in Sacramento, the weather in Phoenix and such like. He tells me about a son who is a roofing contractor, and I tell him about my five kids, all doing quite well, thank you very much.

Finally, I say goodbye and head for camp. I'm feeling good about this meeting and the conversation. Because of my natural shyness, meeting strangers is not an easy thing for me. I resolve to meet as many people as I can this weekend. Everybody has a story to tell.

————

I arrive at the fairgrounds around 11:30 a.m., plenty of time for some red beans and rice and to get a good seat at the Garden Stage venue. I find a seat up front and finish off my beans and rice. People are starting to spread blankets and set up lawn chairs on the grassy area in front of the stage. I strike up a conversation with some folks around me. We talk about Friday's performers—Richard Bona and Diane Reeves. We all agree that they were great. The people behind me are from Pacific Grove and they tell me that the first performer this afternoon is a local guy, John Tucker, who plays frequently in the Monterey area.

I've been to a couple of Saturday afternoon shows in years past and I love them. The afternoon is dedicated to the blues, the roots of jazz. The crowd always gets into it and you spend half of the time on your feet dancing—or trying to.

The show begins and John "Broadway" Tucker comes on like gang busters. He is wearing a black suit, a purple day-glow shirt, a gray fedora, and has a long white scarf thrown around his neck. He begins with a seven-piece acoustic band and does some down home Mississippi Delta stuff. Then he brings on his "Broadway" group, all amped and electric, and they go into more of a South Side Chicago mode. But it's all blues to John Tucker and he belts it out in a big, booming baritone.

Roy Hargrove joins the band for one number. He is Artist in Residence for the weekend and one of the headliners for Saturday night. He has a great tone on the trumpet, bright and crisp, and I'm looking forward to seeing him tonight.

John takes a break between numbers and tells us a story about going home to Greenville, Mississippi, to visit his mom. It is a sweet and touching story and we all love John, and his momma too. Then he sings a song called "I've been lovin' you too long to stop now." It is a real wailer and he finishes down on one knee. It's dynamite stuff! By the time his set is done, we're on our feet, yelling for more.

The crowd has its usual complement of exhibitionists, those who have to be the focus of attention. There is a fifty-something lady, still trim and sexy, who is on her feet and grinding from the first note of John Tucker's set. She is old enough to know better but she just can't resist. Some young guys behind me are cracking jokes. One of them stands up and shouts, "Mom, PLEASE sit down!" It gets a big laugh in our section.

Then there is a cute blonde who drags her boyfriend up in front of the stage to dance. Boyfriend is doing his best to look cool and he's failing miserably. Cute Blonde goes way over the top, somewhere near an "R" rating—mature audiences only. The young guy behind me yells, "I want you to have my baby!" Another big laugh.

The Charles Ford Band, with Robben Ford on guitar and vocals, is up next. There are three Ford brothers in the band and the group is named for their father. I don't expect much from these white guys from Ukiah, but their set kicks butt. They are the hardest working band I've seen and they leave it all on the stage. Again, we are on our feet at the end, giving much love to the Fords.

The Fords are followed by Kevin Moore, stage name Keb' Mo'. He plays guitar and performs most of his songs solo, with occasional accompaniment from a guy playing banjo or guitar. It's down home Mississippi Delta stuff and he has us hanging on every word and every note, like we're sitting in his backyard, sharing songs and telling stories.

Keb' says for a quarter he'll play anything we request. A girl up front says she wants to hear something that will make her cry. Keb' says that will cost a dollar. She runs up to the stage with a dollar and we all laugh. Then Keb' sings:

> *Postman brought me a letter*
> *This is what my letter said*
> *Yeah, postman brought me a letter*
> *This is what my letter said*
> *Said Kevin come home*
> *Cause the girl you loved is dead*

I think the girl got her dollar's worth. The set is an easy, intimate interlude between raging blues bands and it fits perfectly. When he finishes, we give Keb' a standing-O and we truly love him.

To wrap up the afternoon, the next segment is a Detroit Blues Review. The set starts with a rocking seven piece band and they romp through a couple of warm ups. Then it's time for the stars of the revue. First up is Johnny Bassett on guitar and vocals, and he is a master of both. Then comes Joe Weaver who looks and sounds like a preacher. Johnny and Joe rock through a few numbers and they are great.

And then it happens. Onto the stage comes Alberta Adams, seventy-five years young and looking like your favorite grandmother. She has to be helped on stage and she sits at the microphone because she has a bad leg. But when she opens her mouth to sing, out comes this big, strong, booming voice. She belts out a few numbers and in between, she is funny and feisty and bawdy. Throughout her last three songs we are up on our feet, dancing in the aisles. Alberta brings down the house! What a way to end the show.

Time now to get some more red beans and rice, and maybe some of that peach cobbler a la mode I've seen people with. It will be an hour or so before I have to line up for the evening show at Dizzy's Den.

———

I see the line for The Den starting to form early, so I queue up a little after 7:00 p.m. The bill tonight includes three great trumpeters: Dave Douglas, Roy Hargrove, and Nicholas Payton. It promises to be a great show. Both Hargrove and Payton will start out on the main stage, and then move over to Dizzy's Den.

While standing in line, I meet a guy from Florida and a couple from Dallas. The guy from Florida works for Rockwell Electronics. The man and woman from Dallas are both attorneys, though she isn't currently practicing. They have three kids, ages five, four, and eighteen months. She is trim and attractive and I can't believe she has three kids. We chat about kids, schools, baseball, football, golf, and the weather— everything except politics and religion.

By the time they open the doors at 8:00 p.m., the line has serpentined around in several loops. We all stream in and fill the hall to capacity. The announcer comes on to introduce the first act. He tells us that Stanley Turrentine, the great tenor saxophonist, died this week in New York City. It's a surprise to me and everyone around me. I really liked Mr. T. He put out some great albums. Now that he's gone, the record companies will probably reissue his classics. I only hope his family shares in the profits. We observe a moment of silence for Stanley.

Dave Douglas is the first act of the evening. He is a great technical player—good tone, strong attack. But he's a little too avant garde for me. The audience gives him a warm ovation at the end, in typical Monterey fashion.

Next up is Roy Hargrove and he comes out blazing. After several up-tempo numbers, he gives us chills with a beautiful flugelhorn rendition of "Nature Boy," the old Nat Cole ballad. Then it's some funky and some blues, then another beautiful ballad. Finally, he closes the way he opened, with fire! We scream and shout for an encore and he gives us one. At the end of his set, I'm feeling exhausted. It's been a long day.

Nicholas Payton is the last act with his tribute to Louis Armstrong. The band performs songs associated with Armstrong, but with very modern arrangements. It is great stuff. Payton has a wonderful bright, crisp tone on the trumpet, much like Hargrove. But I am pooped and I leave just as the last number begins. On the way to the parking lot, I can hear the crowd cheering for Payton's set.

———

It is a scary ride back to camp. The fog has rolled in through Moss Landing and I have to slow to thirty-five miles per hour and focus on the white line ahead of me. First, I miss the exit off of Highway 1 and I have to double back. Then I miss the turn for the road that leads into the campground. I'm just about to give up and try to make my way back to Castroville to get a motel room when I suddenly find the road to camp. I vow never again: if I see the fog coming in tomorrow night, I'm getting a room in town.

Sunday, September 17, 2000

The sun on the side of my tent wakes me. It is after 7:00 a.m. I didn't hear the siren this morning, so I guess even farm workers get a day off. It is another bright, sunny day; not a trace of last night's fog. I make a feeble attempt at a campfire, which fails miserably, so I decide to shower and shave and head into town for breakfast.

It's eggs and hash browns at Denny's in downtown Monterey. Then I scoot over the hill to Carmel for coffee and a chocolate-striped pretzel at Wisehart's. You didn't think I'd get this close and not go to Wisehart's, did you?

Then it's on to the fairgrounds for the Sunday afternoon shows. I especially want to see the Rio Americano High School band, from the school my three youngest attended. The jazz program has won many awards over the years and produced some fine musicians. I am wearing son Gabe's Rio football tee shirt and my Rio baseball cap so the band will know a fan is present. But the first order of business is to call Matt and see what he thinks of his new car.

I get to the fairgrounds around 11:30 a.m. and head straight for a pay phone. Matt answers the phone and it is really great to hear the excitement in his voice. I also speak to Rachel and Barbara and they fill me in on how they brought off the surprise. I speak to Matt once more and I'm glad I have my sunglasses on so that passersby can't see the tears in my eyes.

―――

Sunday afternoon is devoted to the competition-winning high school bands and vocal groups. I check the program and it looks like once again the place to be is Dizzy's Den.

First on the bill is the Los Angeles School for the Arts Jazz Choir, and they are great. They do vocal renditions of some well-known compositions by John Coltrane, Miles Davis, and others. They even do a two-song tribute to Stanley Turrentine.

It is good to see several black faces in the group. When I was here in 1996, I was shocked to see that the California High School All Star Band had zero black members. I was afraid that all the talented black kids were going into rap and hip-hop. Those fears are set aside by the

L.A. group, the Berkeley High School Jazz Band, and this year's All Star Band.

The Berkeley High Band has a killer trumpet section. The two soloists, Jon Finlayson and Ambrose Akinmusire, are amazing. They are both members of the All Star Band as well. Ambrose gets an especially enthusiastic reaction from the crowd. The Berkeley style is straight-on Bop and they do a great job. (Note: Ambrose Akinmusire went on to become an accomplished recording artist and concert performer.)

At last it is Rio Americano's turn. While they are setting up, I meet the parents of the tenor sax player, Blake Lyman. Blake and two of the Rio trumpet players are also All Star Band members. The parents are bubbling with excitement and pride.

Rio opens with a great arrangement of "Time After Time," then slides into something called "Moby Swing." It is typical of their director Craig Faniani: very tightly arranged, well-rehearsed, and impeccably performed. But somehow I get the impression that Mr. F is just going through the motions.

They go into "Sing, Sing, Sing," which I've heard Rio bands do several times over the years. It is a great arrangement and they perform it well. But it's too short, and wham, they are done and off the stage. I'm left wondering if performing at Monterey has become old hat for Craig and Company. Oh well.

———

I wander over to the Garden Stage and catch the last third of the set by the Brown/Getz Fellows. These are young musicians studying under fellowships established to honor Clifford Brown and Stan Getz. The group consists of piano, bass, drums, and three horns: tenor sax, alto sax, and trumpet.

Their set is straight ahead jazz with strong Bop overtones, and they are amazingly talented musicians. Unfortunately, they have no personality, no stage presence. Many in the crowd are sleeping in the beautiful afternoon sun.

Perhaps there should be a required class for these guys: How to be an Entertainer 101. They should study film of Louis Armstrong and Dizzy Gillespie. Or maybe attend some sessions right here at the festival, such as John Tucker, or Johnny Bassett, or Alberta Adams. Especially Alberta Adams.

———

It is around 5:30 p.m. when the afternoon show ends, time to get something to eat and plot my strategy for the evening. I really want to see the show in the main arena tonight, but I know there is only one way to do that. I will have to leave the grounds and try to buy a ticket from a scalper. The festival has a "no re-entry" policy, so if I leave and can't find a scalper, I can't get back in.

I buy a chicken teriyaki bowl from a Thai food booth and concoct Plan B. If I can't cop a ticket for the main arena, I'll just head back to camp, enjoy the sunset from the observation platform on top of the dunes, and watch the lights come on around the bay. Then I can build a roaring campfire and eat my fill of S'Mores.

I leave the grounds and stroll around to the front gate. I hit a scalper immediately, but he doesn't have main arena tickets to sell. Right in front of the gate, I meet a young couple with a pair of tickets for sale. At first they are reluctant to sell just one of them, but we joke and spar for a while, and they sell me one for a little less than face value. I'm hooked up for the Sunday night show!

———

The Sunday show is scheduled for 7:30 p.m., an hour earlier than the other evening shows, so that everyone can get an early start home. Wayne Shorter and his quintet will be first on the bill. Wayne is the commissioned artist for this year. The Monterey tradition is to commission an original piece of music to be presented either Saturday or Sunday night. Commissioned artists over the years have been the Who's Who of jazz, including Duke Ellington, John Lewis, Charles Mingus, and Dave Brubeck.

Shorter first came to prominence as a young man playing with Art Blakey's Jazz Messengers. Then he was stolen away by Miles Davis for Miles's second great quintet in the mid-sixties. The program notes tell me that Shorter's composition for tonight is based on a piece of Spanish music that Miles Davis handed to him back in the sixties. Miles said,

"Here, see if you can do something with this." The sheet music sat in Wayne's piano bench until recently when he rediscovered it, all yellow and wrinkled. The finished piece is titled "Vendiendo Alegria."

What a great story! From the hand of Miles Davis to Wayne Shorter's piano bench to the Jimmy Lyons Stage at the Monterey Jazz Festival.

Waiting for the show to start, I meet a nice couple form Palo Alto. They are funny and friendly and we chat about the weekend and their favorite performers. Several of the people surrounding us join in and I realize that they all know each other from years past. They all renew their tickets every year. I am the lone interloper, thanks to the couple who sold me their ticket.

The show gets underway and Wayne Shorter comes on with a group composed of piano, drums, bass, and a percussionist who sits behind an amazing wall of congas, bongos, gourds, shakers, chimes, and every other percussion instrument you can think of.

Wayne has me worried. The first two numbers make me wonder if, at age sixty-seven, he has lost his chops. Not to worry: he was just warming up. By the fourth number it is clear: the chops are still there in full force.

He brings on the Monterey Chamber Jazz Orchestra, about twenty members strong. I see trombones, French horns, bassoons, clarinets, saxophones, and almost every type of woodwind you can imagine. They perform a piece for openers, kind of a warm-up, and the collective sound is great.

Then they launch into the "Vendiendo Alegria." It is rich and interesting with a strong Spanish flavor and I'm loving it, sure that I am hearing something memorable. All too soon it is over. We give Wayne and the orchestra a standing ovation in the warm, loving Monterey way. Then the legend leaves the stage. I wish him many happy returns.

During the break, most of my seatmates head out for a drink or something to eat. I notice a black couple standing a few rows ahead of me. He looks to be in his sixties; she's maybe fifty-something. They are both tall and elegant looking and I think about wandering over to strike up a conversation. But my old shyness returns with a vengeance and I stand mute.

The lights dim and guitarist Pat Metheny is introduced. He leads off with his trio that includes Larry Grenadier on bass and Bill Stewart on drums. They sail through three tunes with ease. Then Pat brings on tenor saxophonist Michael Brecker, an old collaborator, and things start to get interesting. Everything is amped, including Brecker's microphone pick up, and they achieve some great effects. Brecker contributes some amazing solos, building tension until you think the horn is going to explode, then resolving it and giving us some much-needed relief.

To close out the set, they bring on Larry Goldings on the Hammond B3 organ and Grenadier takes a break. They make it through one number just fine. Then they launch into a bluesy vamp and it is clear that this is going to feature Goldings on the B3. But as he starts into his solo, something goes wrong with the sound pick-up for the organ. Technicians scurry around the stage but to no avail. Goldings stands up, throws down a towel and stomps off the stage. The band stops and they stand there dumbfounded for a moment. Pat Metheny takes the microphone, apologizes to the crowd and says they are just trying to do the best they can.

Then something amazing happens: all through the crowd people are leaping to their feet, clapping and shouting encouragement. I'm thinking, *Only in Monterey.*

Grenadier comes back on stage and they go into their closing number. Except for the Goldings snafu they've been great, and when they finish we stand and shout and whistle, demanding an encore.

Metheny and Brecker trot back out and Metheny goes into an astounding version of "Summertime." I've never heard it played this way. To describe it as intense would be an understatement. It is so intense I'm expecting the guitar to break. Then Brecker comes in with and equally intense, highly amped solo. And finally they bring it down to a beautiful, haunting restatement of the theme: "Summertime, and the livin' is easy."

The audience is hushed until the last note dies, and then we explode. Metheny and Brecker embrace on stage and then stand side by side, grinning from ear to ear while the ovation washes over them. They wave goodbye and they are gone.

And so the festival ends. I turn to say goodbye to my friends from Palo Alto but they are gone. As I head out of the arena, everywhere you look people are hugging, saying have a great year, see you next September. It is like the end of a family reunion.

Out on the grounds on the way to the parking lot, the buzz is about Wayne Shorter—some liked it, some didn't—and it is about the

Goldings tantrum. But mainly it is about Metheny and Brecker and their performance of "Summertime."

———

I stop on the way back to camp to fill up with gas and to buy a newspaper. I glance at it quickly and, lo and behold, on the front page is a picture from the Saturday afternoon show. It is a shot of the fifty-something lady dancing her buns off. "Mom, PLEASE sit down!"

It is an easy ride back to camp. Not a trace of fog. I'm in the tent around midnight.

Monday, September 18, 2000

Happy Birthday to Me,
Happy Birthday to Me,
Happy Birthday, Dear Chucky,
Happy Birthday to Me.

The 7:00 a.m. siren sounds on the strawberry farm. I lay in the tent for a while thinking back on the weekend. I think I have figured out why I was so reluctant to get going on Friday morning. This weekend represents a bridge for me, from my old life to a new one that isn't fully defined. When I go home, my career at Roseville Telephone will be virtually over, and before long I hope to be settled in my new gig as a consultant. I guess it is normal to be apprehensive about major changes like this.

After a while, I climb out of the tent to discover that the campground is nearly deserted. Only two other tents are visible. I am resolved to make a serious attempt at a campfire this morning. I picked up the *Monterey Herald* on the way back last night, so I have the whole Sunday paper to help get the fire started. The fire gets going pretty well and I make some coffee. Then I break out the fixin's for S'Mores. Hey, it's my birthday and if I want S'Mores for breakfast, so be it. Besides, there is nobody close enough to see me and cast aspersions. It may not be Martha Stewart living, but then again, maybe it is.

Chuck: You know, Martha, the secret to a great S'Mores is in using only the best ingredients.

Martha: Hmmm, I see. And what are the best ingredients, Chuck?

Chuck: Well, you have to start with a fine graham cracker. Nabisco makes a nice honey graham. Marshmallows, of course, are pretty generic, though I'm partial to Stay Puff.

Martha: Really?

Chuck: That's right, Martha. Now here is the important part: the chocolate bar. Some folks try to use big, thick pieces of chocolate, but that's a mistake. The classic Hershey Bar is by far the best.

Martha: You don't say—

Chuck: It's true, it's true. Here's another key: do not burn the marshmallow! You want it to be a nice golden brown on the outside and melted on the inside. There now, Martha, try this one.

Martha: Mmmmm, Chuck, that is fabulous!

After three or four S'Mores, I have globs of marshmallow in my mustache. No wonder my daughter Rachel calls it a "flavor saver."

I decide to spend the day walking in the footsteps of my idol, John Steinbeck. I'll spend some time on Cannery Row, then maybe go to the Steinbeck Center in Salinas, and finish with a trip up to Fremont's Peak.

By 9:00 a.m., I'm packed and headed out of the campground. I stop near the ranger station for one last look at the beach. The white, sandy sweep of it is magnificent. I wonder if you can walk from Monterey all the way to the Boardwalk in Santa Cruz? It would be fun to try.

———

On Cannery Row, I have my choice of parking places at the curb. A Monday in mid-September is obviously a good time to be here, if you like to avoid the crowds. I wander down the street to Steinbeck Plaza and stand in front of the bronze bust of my hero. The plaque under the bust is cast with the opening paragraph of *Cannery Row*.

> Cannery Row in Monterey in California is a poem, a stink, a grating noise, a quality of light, a tone, a habit, a nostalgia, a dream. Cannery Row is the gathered and scattered, tin and iron and rust and splintered wood, chipped pavement and weedy lots and junk heaps, sardine canneries of corrugated iron, honky tonks, restaurants and whore houses, and little crowded groceries, and laboratories and flophouses.

The book caused a stink and a grating noise when it was published in 1945. The locals were angry at the way they were portrayed. Now that description is honored and marketed in this commercial plaza. One doesn't have to think very hard to know what Steinbeck would think of all this. But it is remarkable how much of the description still fits.

I stroll further down the street to 800 Cannery Row where Dr. Ed Ricketts's lab still stands. I'm surprised someone hasn't had the bright idea to spruce up the place and charge admission for tours. They've probably done the math and decided there was no profit to be taken.

I walk across the street and peer into Lee Chong's market. They sell antiques there now. I step back and try to picture where the Bear Flag Inn stood, and the vacant lot with the abandoned boiler that Suzy turned into a home, complete with lace curtains.

What David S. Ward did to *Cannery Row* in the 1982 movie still irks me. What a giant pair of *cojones* it must take to rewrite John Steinbeck! Someday I hope somebody tries again and gets it right. It wouldn't be hard. Just combine *Cannery Row* and *Sweet Thursday* into a single narrative and stay true to the story line.

I look for a place to sit down and write in this journal and I spy Ghirardelli's Ice Cream Parlor. It's pretty close to noon now, a respectable time for a hot fudge sundae. After all, it's my birthday. I sit on the narrow terrace overhanging a sandy beach. Little waves are splashing in and some sandpipers run to and fro, staying just beyond the wavelets. It is very pleasant sitting there. The sundae is good and I fill many pages in this journal before I realize over an hour has passed. It's time to go.

I decide to forego the Steinbeck Center. I've been there before and I'll go again, but that will be another day. Besides, Fremont's Peak is on the way home, just off of Highway 156. I head out of town on Highway 1, leaving Monterey and the beautiful bay and the white sand in my rearview mirror.

———

The turnoff for Fremont's Peak is clearly marked and I start the gentle eleven-mile drive up to the state park at the top of the mountain. From the parking lot below the peak, you can see the U.S. flag flying from a pole at the very pinnacle. This is the first spot in California where the U.S. flag was raised, much to the chagrin of the Mexican government that claimed California at the time.

From the parking lot, there is a trail that winds around and up to the peak. By the time I near the top, I'm breathing pretty hard. It is a warm day and I've broken a good sweat, too. I scramble up the last twenty feet or so of granite rock and I'm standing at the foot of the flagpole. The view is incredible, nearly three hundred and sixty degrees. I sit down on the monument at the base of the flagpole, open my backpack and pull out my dog-eared copy of *Travels with Charley*. Steinbeck describes visiting this very spot with his dog Charley on his swing through Northern California.

> ...Here on these high rocks my memory myth repaired itself. Charley, having explored the area, sat at my feet, his fringed ears blowing like laundry on a line. His nose, moist with curiosity, sniffed the wind-borne pattern of a hundred miles.
>
> "You wouldn't know, my Charley, that right down there, in that little valley, I fished for trout with your namesake, my Uncle Charley. And over there—see where I'm pointing—my mother shot a wildcat. Straight down there, forty miles away, our family ranch was—old starvation ranch. Can you see that darker place there? Well, that's a tiny canyon with a clear and lovely stream bordered with wild azaleas and fringed with big oaks. On one of those oaks my father burned his name with a hot iron together with the name of the girl he loved. In the long years the bark grew over the burn and covered it. And just a little while ago, a man cut that oak for firewood and his splitting wedge uncovered my father's name and the man sent it to me. In the spring, Charley, when the valley is carpeted with blue lupines like a flowery sea, there's the smell of heaven up here, the smell of heaven."
>
> I printed it once more on my eyes, south, west, and north, and then we hurried away from the permanent and changeless past where my mother is

always shooting a wildcat and my father is always
burning his name with his love.

What a beautiful passage, filled with love of family and home. I
try to guess the whereabouts of the canyons and streams that Steinbeck
was pointing out to Charley, but it is only guesswork. It is an amazing
thing for me to be sitting here knowing he was here in this exact spot. I
try to drink in the view: Monterey Bay, the Salinas Valley, and the low
mountains, and I curse myself for not bringing a camera.

After a while it's time to head back down the trail to the parking
lot. I make up my mind to climb the peak again exactly two years from
today, on my sixtieth birthday. I'll even bring a split of Champagne and
drink a toast to John Steinbeck for all the reading pleasure he's given me.

I think about what might happen between now and September
2002, and what I might hope for. My first wish is that all of my
children continue on their current paths, which are straight and true
and successful. I think of all the members of our family and I wish for
continued good health and happiness. As for me, I just hope I can make
the climb at sixty.

On the way out of the park, I stop at the self-registration station.
The day-use fee is posted at one dollar. I stuff several dollars in one of
the registration envelopes and on the outside I write: "In memory of
John Steinbeck and Stanley Turrentine." That will give 'em something
to think about.

At last, I point the car down the mountain road. It is time to cross
that bridge and get back to reality.

Afterword – June, 2013

September of 2000 was a long time ago and it's amazing to think about what we've been through since then. Less than a year later, we would experience the attacks of September 11, 2001, followed shortly by the wars in Afghanistan and Iraq. Certain phrases and names would enter our daily conversation: ground zero, Osama bin Laden, Al Qaeda, Shock and Awe, weapons of mass destruction, Abu Ghraib, Tora Bora, and on and on. The list continues to grow, but it would have been nice if it had ended with Abbottabad.

An African-American would be elected president—twice—and we would debate the pros and cons of something called Obamacare. Every day in the news we would hear the names Boehner, Pelosi, Reid, and McConnell, and we would watch them take the Congress of the United States to an all-time low, at least in terms of public approval. We would also debate climate change as we witnessed hurricanes Katrina and Sandy and watched tornados lay waste to towns across the heartland.

A housing market bubble would burst, leading to a near-global financial meltdown. We would learn that some companies—and their executives—are too big to fail, while millions of Americans were thrown out of work. The term Great Recession will eventually take its place in history, along with the Great Depression of the 1930s.

The plague of mass murder by deranged individuals continued unabated. We have no answers, at least none the NRA will buy. And so the procession continues, from Columbine, to Virginia Tech, to Tucson, to Aurora, to Newtown, to Santa Monica, and points in between. It doesn't matter if you are a congresswoman, a first grader, or a spectator on Boylston Street in Boston, it's open season.

And what of our personal history? If you are like me, it's been a mixture of the good and the bad, the miraculous and the tragic. The best news, at least in my family, is that a whole new generation of grandchildren, great grandchildren, nieces, nephews, and cousins have come along to brighten our lives. We may worry about what we are leaving them, but they will be loved and doted upon, just as their parents before them.

I never did go back to the Monterey Jazz Festival, never again climbed Fremont's Peak to drink that promised champagne toast. But it's on my bucket list. And guess what: the climb really isn't that hard.

V.

Bro. Dick
A Remembrance

For all the kids in the family.
When you read it, you'll understand why.

Preface...

It was the morning of March 5, 1988, and I was just settling down with a cup of coffee and the morning paper when the phone rang. It was my sister-in-law Monica, calling with the news that we all knew was coming. My brother Dick had been admitted to American River Hospital during the night and he wasn't expected to make it through the day. She knew I'd want to be there and she suggested that I come as soon as possible. There was no way to know how long he would live.

It had been a long hard battle—the radiation treatments, the chemotherapy, the long list of complications, and the even longer list of specialists and their procedures—but now all that was over. The regimen now was to give him as much morphine as needed to keep him quiet and as comfortable as possible under the circumstances, and hopefully, to let him die in peace.

I showered and dressed and headed for the hospital as quickly as possible, thinking all the while about my brother and the many twists and turns our lives had taken. I thought about my daughters Cheryl and Kim, now in their mid-twenties. Dick was an important part of their lives until they were eight and nine years old. After that came my brother's marriage, and then my divorce and remarriage, the result being that they just didn't see him that much anymore. I thought of my three youngest—Matt, Rachel, and Gabe—and the fact that they barely knew him. In fact, none of them knew him the way that I did. That bothered me—a lot! Nearly twenty years later, it still bothers me.

And so, here I am, setting out to right that wrong, to try to tell my kids and anyone else who may read this all the things I remember about my brother. If he's watching me now, I'm sure he has that little smirk on his face, the one he used to get just before he'd stick a pin in whatever balloon I was inflating. Well, brother, go ahead and smirk and laugh and skewer me with a pointed remark. I don't care. I'm going to tell the whole world all about Richard Louis "Dick" Spooner. There's no stopping me now.

C.W.S.
November 7, 2007

Bro. Dick and Bro. Chas...

I should start by explaining the title: "Bro. Dick." When I moved to Minnesota in the spring of 1962, Dick and I started an exchange of letters that went on for nearly three years. It was a time when long distance phone rates were still considered high and you made long distance calls only for family emergencies and special occasions. At least that was our family culture, coming from parents who vividly remembered the Great Depression and the rationing of the war years. I realize that this is probably hard to grasp in the era of cell phones and the Internet, but in those days, people actually sat down with pen and paper and wrote letters to one another.

In the late fifties, one of the landmark shows on TV was *Maverick*, the prototypical western starring James Garner and Jack Kelley. It's the show that launched Garner's career and it became an institution at our home in Vallejo. We'd all gather in the living room around the old black-and-white TV every Sunday evening to watch *Maverick*. As our father liked to say, we'd wind up with powder burns and saddle sores.

The Maverick boys always referred to each other as Brother Brett and Brother Bart. So when Dick and I began our correspondence in 1962, we would sign our letters with "Bro. Dick," or "Bro. Chas." Corny, right? Hey, we thought it was pretty cool.

My brother and I both fancied ourselves as authors and we'd work hard at one-upmanship, seeing who could write the best letter. It was good fun. I can't tell you how much I looked forward to opening the mailbox and seeing my brother's fine handwriting on an envelope inside. I only wish I had the foresight to save all those letters.

And so, there you have it: the genesis of the title of this composition. It's all about Bro. Dick.

He doesn't look anything like you...

Let me start by describing my brother, at least to tell you the way our family saw him. You have to understand that we all adored him, so this is hardly an objective assessment. There was just something that drew you to him. Maybe it was the gleaming white smile, or the piercing blue eyes, or the curly-wavy blonde hair that was always neatly trimmed, or the fact that at an even six feet tall, he always looked slim and fit at about 150 lbs. More likely it was the keen sense of humor and the easy laugh, or the highly developed skill at recognizing BS and calling it to your attention immediately.

Until Dick was well into his forties, it seemed like he had discovered the fountain of youth. He never seemed to age. I remember going to the San Francisco airport with Dick and my brother-in-law Ken. We were there to meet someone (can't remember who) and we arrived early, so we went into the bar to kill time until the plane landed. I was 21 at the time, my brother was 30, and Ken was a few years older than Dick. The bartender came over to take our order, took a hard look at the three of us, and asked only my brother for his ID. Amazing!

My friends all had a common reaction when they met my brother. If I heard this once, I'll bet I heard it a hundred times: "That's your brother? He doesn't look anything like you. He's nice looking." It's a funny thing, but I never resented that remark. In fact, I'd tell the story myself and it always got a good laugh. It was the truth, and I was proud to have a handsome older brother.

I would sum it up by saying that he was intelligent, well read, witty, interested in a wide range of subjects, and always up for a good debate. He was also hard working, grounded, and devoted to his family.

For me, it was pretty simple: he was my idol.

The consummate tease...

When I was little, my brother knew all the buttons to push that would send me into fits of frustration. As a matter of fact, he could have that effect on our sister Edna as well. To put it simply, he was the consummate tease.

Dick was nine years older than me and my earliest memories were from the age of four or thereabouts. As the baby of the family, I was spoiled rotten by my parents, and by sister Edna as well. Which is to say that I was the perfect target for my brother to take me down a notch or two. My Mom liked to dress me up in special outfits—little white sailor suits with white shoes, things like that—and trot me off to have my picture taken. I'd walk around thinking I was hot stuff until Dick would lay into me with the well-executed tease. He'd have me pitching a fit in no time.

The all-time classic was the Cowboy Suit incident. Yes, I was into the cowboy thing as a little guy, including the full-on outfit—the hat, the shirt, the bandana, the vest, the chaps, the spurs, and of course the holster and cap gun set. I remember standing in the dining room by the kitchen door and Dick was across the table from me and he was really giving it to me, making me feel utterly ridiculous in my cowboy outfit. Finally, I'd had enough. I whipped out my gun, reared back and threw it at him as hard as I could. Of course he simply ducked and the gun crashed into the wall and fell to the floor in two or three pieces. Whenever I watch *Bull Durham* and it comes to that scene outside the bar where Nuke throws the baseball at Crash and misses and takes out the window in the door, I always think of my brother. Ball four!

The gun hit the wall barrel first, leaving a neat little hole in the plaster. Dad got involved at this point and warmed my backside with a well-placed swat. I couldn't help but notice that everyone else—my Mom, my sister, and especially Bro. Dick—were trying hard not to laugh. Which, of course, added to my discomfort.

Dad did a curious thing in the wake of this little episode. He could have patched that gun barrel sized hole in the wall with plaster or spackle, but he never did. Every time the room was painted through the years, he'd just dab a little paint in the hole and move on. It was as if he wanted it there to remind me. After a while, it got to be a little embarrassing. People always asked about that damn hole in the wall. And there'd always be someone around to tell the story.

As I got a little older and came to appreciate my brother a little more, I was glad I didn't hit him with the cap gun. There were far more subtle ways to get even.

Of paperboys and beer breath...

My brother had a neighborhood paper route all through his teens. In those days, your friendly news carrier was considered an independent businessman. Not only did he deliver the paper, both morning and evening editions, he also went door to door each month collecting for the service. From the money he collected, he had to pay the distributor for his papers. If he was able to collect from every customer, it worked out pretty well, especially when tips were figured in. The catch was that not everyone paid, at least not promptly. It was a great education in business and finance and record keeping and the value of hard work. The paperboy was right up there with the postman: nothing could stay him from his appointed rounds.

I would hear the alarm clock at about five in the morning, and my mom in the kitchen, making breakfast for my dad and my brother. On days when the rain was pounding on the roof and making gurgling noises in the downspouts, I remember thinking *my brother is nuts*. Then I'd roll over and go back to sleep.

I have to say here that lots of paperboys came and went. Dick Spooner, however, was another story. He kept it going for years, earning money for clothes and entertainment, and if memory serves, eventually putting a down payment on his first car. He was that good.

Our front porch and driveway became newsboy central. The distributor would drop off bound stacks of papers for several carriers and they'd all gather at our house to fold their papers and stuff them into their bags. For those of you who have never seen one, the paperboy's bag was like a serape that fit over your head and shoulders and had pouches in front and back to carry the newspapers. Folding the papers and packing them in the bag was an art, one that has been lost in the modern era. There were no rubber bands available during the war years; rubber was a scarce commodity. Instead, paperboys learned an array of folding techniques, depending on the size of the paper. There was the roll-and-crimp, the three-cornered-box fold, and so on. If you were a skilled carrier, you could ride your bike down the street, reach into your bag, and with a quick backhand toss, land the paper neatly on the customer's front porch.

Our Dad rode the bus to and from work and he'd arrive home each evening just as the guys were loading their bags and about to head out on their routes. I had a ritual that I shared with my parents: my Mom and Dad would sit down at the table in the dining room and share a cold beer, and they'd always pour me an inch or so in a juice glass. Actually, it was a little glass that Kraft cheese spread came in and we'd save them to use as juice glasses.

One evening, after I had my beer with my parents, I went outside to harass my brother's friends. Mike Lyons was one of Dick's best buddies and I especially liked to bug him. So he picked me up and was throwing me around over his shoulders when suddenly he got a whiff of my breath. "Hey, this kid's got beer on his breath," he yelled. And that's how my cover was blown.

When I was about five, I got my first two-wheeler. I had a hard time reaching the pedals, so my Dad cut some wood blocks and bolted them on to make it easier for me. As soon as I learned to ride, I started asking Dick to take me with him on his route. He wanted none of that. After all, this was his business and he didn't need a kid brother tagging along. But I kept it up until he finally caved in and agreed to let me come. I think Mom interceded on my behalf as well. Anyway, Dick made it clear that he wasn't going to wait for me. I'd darn well better keep up or he'd leave me behind and I could find my own way home.

We were clipping along down the sidewalk on Irwin Street, my brother setting a brisk pace, papers flying out and landing on the porches, cruising along like a well-oiled machine. That was my brother. For my part, I was pumping as hard and fast as I could and barely managing to keep up. Then it happened. At one of the houses, the paper hit a group of three or four milk bottles left on the porch for the milkman. I heard the sound of breaking glass as the bottles scattered, and then my brother hit the brakes and came to a quick stop in front of me. Before I could react, I crashed into the back of his bike.

You have to understand this about Bro. Dick: he was a pretty mellow guy ninety-nine percent of the time. But when he got mad, he got really, really mad, and he could swear like a sailor. Not unusual for a guy who grew up in a Navy town. Anyway, I crashed into his back wheel and went flying, and my brother let loose with a stream of expletives that turned the air blue. He regrouped quickly, made sure I was okay—nothing more than wounded pride—then went to knock on the customer's door and explain the accident.

Needless to say, that was the first and only time I went along on the paper route.

The heart failure kid...

Dick was a pretty good ballplayer, a long-legged outfielder who could cover a lot of ground in centerfield. I know this because I insisted on tagging along with him when he played sandlot ball. The Greater Vallejo Recreation District (GVRD) ran a summer program down at Steffan Manor School, just a block from home. Part of that program was a baseball league set up with several divisions based on age. There was the underweight division for the guys ten and under, and then the middleweights for the eleven- and twelve-year-olds. The upper division was—you guessed it—the heavyweights, up to age fifteen if memory serves. There were teams representing schools and playgrounds all around the city, and for a seat-of-the-pants organization, the program was well run and the games very competitive. There were some fine ballplayers around Vallejo who got their start in sandlot ball.

I loved going down to the school with Dick and watching the guys practice or play games. It was just a great place to hang out. The GVRD had two classrooms on the north wing of the school, one for arts and crafts and general activities, and one with two ping-pong tables that were constantly busy. Outside on the courtyard, there were paddle tennis and basketball courts, and then out away from the classrooms were the baseball fields. The staff usually consisted of two or three people, one of them being the designated baseball coach. Typically the coach was a high school or college student looking to make some spending money during the summer months. Not so at Steffan. We had Mr. Boyle.

Mr. Boyle was a retiree who loved kids and loved baseball and viewed his GVRD job as a way to enjoy both. He had a face like a map of Ireland and his accent told you right away that he hailed from Boston. He was a big, heavyset man with a bulbous nose and a rosy complexion. My guess is that he liked to chase down a shot of Old Bushmill's with a pint of Guinness, but that's only a guess. Listening to Mr. Boyle talk was very much like listening to Casey Stengel at his best, one random thought leading to another, connected only by the love of the game.

I'd bug my brother to let me come along down to the playground and he'd eventually relent and take me along, probably under pressure from Mom. My favorite things to do were to cheer at the top of my lungs for the Steffan Manor Heavyweights and then join in the team huddles so that I could listen to Mr. Boyle hold forth.

The ball field at Steffan was terrible! The ground slopped from south to north and over the years, all the topsoil had washed down to a narrow band at the north end. The field itself was pure hardpan. If you were wise, you wore a mouthpiece to protect your teeth from ground balls. That's how bad it was. But hey, that was sandlot baseball.

I remember one season-ending game that must have been for the city championship or something, because a nice crowd turned out to watch and the atmosphere was electric. Late in the game, the other team put a couple of guys on base with two outs and their big hitter coming to the plate. Well, Big Hitter uncorked a long, high drive to left center, heading out to where the ball field ended and the school playground began, way out toward the monkey bars and swings. You could tell by the crack of the bat that he got all of it. I saw Dick turn and take off on the dead run and I was sure he didn't have a chance to catch the ball. His best hope was to chase it down and get it back to the infield before the hitter rounded the bases and scored.

Now this is a stretch, but if you ever saw Joe DiMaggio glide across centerfield in Yankee Stadium, then you know what it was like to watch my brother run. There he was, flying after that ball, heading toward the monkey bars, and then he reached up with his left hand and snared the ball in the web of his glove. From way back behind home plate, you could clearly see half the ball protruding from his glove. It was the best catch I had ever seen. It still is.

Steffan won the game and Mr. Boyle was ecstatic! He gathered the team around him and went into a long dissertation about what a great game it was, calling out all the guys who had contributed to the victory, rambling on in his best Stengelese. Somewhere near the end, he got to Dick's catch: "... and then there's Spoonah out there in cenahfield, givin' me heart failyah..."

The Spooners are a family of storytellers. There is a rich tradition of oral history that requires the passing along of classic stories from generation to generation. The story of this game and Mr. Boyle's speech became part of our family history. Nobody enjoyed telling it more than me. And nobody enjoyed hearing it more than Bro. Dick.

Where's Dickie?...

This chapter is going to be hard to write, because I don't want anyone to think that we didn't love the Sanders—my Aunt Marie, Uncle Ed, cousins Louis and Celia, and Louis's son John—because we did love them dearly. Let's just say they had this odd habit of dropping by the house unannounced and we weren't always ready for them, especially Bro. Dick.

Aunt Marie was the oldest of my Mom's sisters and she fancied herself the matriarch of the family. She was very heavy, to the point where it was difficult for her to walk and climb stairs. Uncle Ed, on the other hand, was tall and lean and Lincolnesque, and he had this profound bass voice that resonated through the room. He was a greeter at the church they attended and someone once told me that he was known as Whisperin' Ed because you could hear him greeting new arrivals in the foyer no matter where you sat in the large sanctuary. Louis was built like his father and shared his wonderful voice. He worked on the shipyard, but built a reputation for himself as an actor in the local theater company, and as the public address announcer at Corbus Field, the high school football stadium. And then there was John, tall like his grandfather and father, but always something of a lost man-child. All things considered, they were an odd little group.

If Dick was at home when the Sanders did one of their pop-ins, he would respectfully sit through a visit with our Aunt and Uncle. But if Louis and John were along for the ride, my brother just couldn't handle it. Maybe it was because they insisted on calling him Dickie, or maybe it was just his low tolerance for strange ducks. Either way, he would go to great lengths to make himself scarce.

Dick would see their car pull up out in front of the house and he'd exclaim "Oh, shit! Tell them I went out. I'm not here!" Then he'd head out the back of the house to find a place to hide. They'd come in, booming their hearty hello's, and immediately begin with, "Where's Dickie? We wanna say hi to Dickie?" They'd noticed his car out front so they knew he was around somewhere. Then it was time for me to have some fun. "Gee, I don't know where he is. He was here just a minute ago." With that, Louis and John would lurch off on a search through the house, calling out "Dickie, Dickie, how are ya' Dickie." They'd even go out into the garage and the backyard, trying to track down my brother. He'd be crouched down behind some old furniture up in the attic, or out behind Dad's storage shed at the back of the lot. If necessary, he'd jump the fence and escape out onto Cedar Street. Through all this, I'd be laughing so hard my sides hurt. After a half hour or so, they'd be on their way, and my brother would come slinking back into the house.

"What the hell did you tell them, for God's sake! They almost came up into the attic after me."

"I just told 'em you were around here somewhere."

"Goddamit, tell 'em I'm gone, I went to the store, I went out with a friend. Just don't tell 'em I'm here!"

We played this scene many times with only slight variations in the script. It was always a great laugh. I told you there were subtle ways to get even for all the teasing I had to absorb. This was only one of them.

Sundays with Airman Spooner...

Dick joined the Air Force when I was about ten. I remember many conversations at home among the adults saying what a fine thing this was for my brother to do, serving his country and all. Dad was really proud of him, even though he would have preferred the Navy.

It turned out that Dick's basic training assignment was at Camp Parks, near Dublin in the Livermore Valley; and so began a series of five or six Sundays when my Mom and Dad and I would drive from Vallejo to spend the afternoon with Dick. We'd cross the Carquinez Bridge, pick up Highway 4 over to Martinez, then head down a beautiful two-lane road lined with walnut trees through towns with quaint sounding names: Concord, Walnut Creek, Pacheco, Danville, San Ramon, and finally Dublin. Next to Marin County, I thought the Diablo and Livermore valleys were the prettiest places I'd ever seen. They're still beautiful today, but a lot has changed since the early fifties, and not all for the good.

It was funny at first to see my brother with his hair cut really, really short, wearing his olive drab fatigues and the little square top fatigue cap. He looked like a blonde Beetle Bailey. The best part of the trip was eating dinner in the mess hall. I thought the food was great. All in all, it was a good time for our family. Mom and Dad were bursting with pride, Dick seemed to be doing well, we met several guys from his barracks and they all seemed to be nice. It was a great way to spend a Sunday.

We'd leave for Vallejo before it got too dark and when we got home, Dad would say, "Let's go bowling." So off we'd go to the Miracle Bowl on Tennessee Street to bowl a few games. Sometimes my Uncle Max would join us. It was great fun.

Basic training was over in six weeks and then Dick shipped out to Biloxi, Mississippi. It was only six weeks, but those Sundays are a warm, peaceful memory for me. It was a good time for our little family unit.

Weiser's wake...

Warren McManus was Dick's best friend, but we didn't dare call him Warren. To everyone in the neighborhood he was Weiser (Wee-zur). He lived across the street from my friend Dillon up on Jennings Street and all of us little kids loved him. He was just a great guy. His mom and dad (we called them Momma Mac and Daddy Mac) were like a second set of parents to my brother.

Our dad would cast a pretty critical eye on anyone we brought home, and if he saw things he didn't like, we were sure to hear about it. On the other hand, if he took a liking to your friend, that person could always count on a hearty welcome and a slap on the back when he came through the front door. Dad loved Weiser and he was always welcome in our home.

In the forties and fifties and on through the Vietnam years, a young man was accountable for military service. Either you enlisted, were drafted, had a student deferment, or there was a documented reason why you could not serve. Whatever the case, you were accountable. When my brother and his friends hit the magic age—eighteen or nineteen—they began to make their choices. Dick and his friend Jerry enlisted in the Air Force. Weiser chose the Marines and headed off to Camp Pendleton for basic training.

I can't remember the year, but I know it was around the Christmas holiday season, and all the guys were going to be home on leave. Weiser was on his way home when somehow his car went off the road and rolled over several times and he was killed. The whole neighborhood went into mourning, but especially my brother. Dick was devastated.

He visited Momma Mac and Daddy Mac to pay his condolences and they invited him to Weiser's wake. Dick had never been to an Irish wake and had no idea what to expect. That evening he put on his dress blue uniform, braced himself, and set out for the McManus's home. What happened there changed my brother in a very profound way. The house was filled with food and drink, there was laughter everywhere, glasses were raised and stories were told, and the Irish whiskey flowed like a bubbling spring. It was a party!

Dick came away thoroughly shaken. He wasn't prepared for a party and it took him several days to recover. We talked about it many times in the years that followed and I know that the experience shaped his beliefs about death and dying. He came to see Weiser's wake as a celebration of his life, and that's exactly as it should have been. Sad funerals, Dick would say, are only for the living. That person you loved has passed on to a better place, and their life and that passage should be celebrated. He came to believe that graveyards and gravesites were also only for those left behind. Many times he would tell me, "The person you loved is not in that grave, Charlie."

As he grew older, I don't remember Dick being involved with any specific church and I think he was pretty skeptical about organized religion. That doesn't mean that he wasn't a spiritual person, or that he didn't believe in God. Quite the contrary! Someone (I can never remember who) said: "We are spiritual beings having a brief physical experience." I think Dick would have seized on that statement, and I think that is what he ultimately took away from Weiser's wake.

This is not to say that my brother was right, or to questions anyone's beliefs. I think we all have to come to grips with these questions for ourselves. I only know that our conversations had a major impact on me as I was growing up and formulating my own belief system. It also explains something that may seem a little strange: in the twenty years since my brother's death, I have never visited his grave. Not even once. My heart tells me he isn't there.

The baseball connection...

When I started playing Little League baseball, suddenly the tables were turned. Where I had spent my early years tagging along after my brother, now he was busy following me. Dick became my biggest fan. Well, maybe number three, right behind Mom and Dad. He tried to see as many games as possible, especially when I played on All Star teams and we traveled to tournaments which were generally somewhere in the Central Valley. Dick was stationed at Mather AFB in Sacramento during my Little League days and he'd bring some of his friends and show up wherever we were playing. I'd like to think that we put on a pretty good show most of the time. At least we were seldom ever boring.

When I was ten, Dick followed our All Star team to Menlo Park where we won all of our games. I didn't play much, but that was okay. I was perfectly happy to let my older teammates carry the load. Then it was on to Marysville where things got really interesting. I was called in to pitch the last two innings of a one-run game which we eventually won. Our winning run was scored on a balk call, a call made by an umpire from Vallejo no less. Then Mom passed out in the stands and had to be taken to the hospital in an ambulance. She was okay, just too much heat and too much excitement. A Vallejo sportswriter said I pitched like I had ice water in my veins. And over on page two was a little article with the headline, "Baseball Too Much For Mom." What an adventure!

The next year, in a tournament in Stockton, I pitched a no-hitter. Pretty cool for an eleven year-old! And of course, Mom and Dad and Bro. Dick were there, cheering me on. No ambulances or hospitals on that trip.

When I was twelve, my brother brought his Air Force friends, Jim Bowers and Paul Kilty, to see us play. I vaguely remember that we were playing in Stockton again, but I clearly remember that it was very hot. Seems like it always worked out that way for Vallejo teams. We'd grown up in the cool North Bay with temperatures between sixty-five and seventy-five in the summer. The hot Central Valley always killed us.

Kilty was from Boston and had a very heavy accent. My brother used to challenge him to say things like, "I left my car keys in my khakis." Of course, it came out, "I left my cah keys in my cahkis." My brother, the tease.

I was the starting pitcher and I really wanted to have a great game for Dick and his buddies. As it turned out, I just didn't have it that day. No zip on the fastball, couldn't find the strike zone. When the coach took me out, we were down 5 to 0 and I was devastated. He sent me to centerfield where I spent most of the time drying my eyes on my sleeve. Henry Rimmer came in to pitch and held the other team in check. Dick loved to watch Henry pitch because he had a silky smooth wind-up and a pretty leg kick and a sharp little curve ball that broke very late. When Henry was getting that curve in the strike zone he was really tough to hit.

Lo and behold, I hit a three-run home run in fifth inning and we were right back in the game. But it was too late and we wound up losing 5 – 3. After the game, I felt rotten for pitching poorly and letting my teammates down. The tears just kept coming and my sleeve got really wet.

A couple of years ago, fall of 2005, I was sitting at my desk one day and the phone rang. It was Jim Bowers. He had lost touch with Dick over the years and didn't know that he had died. We chatted for a while and I got the impression that Jim was going through some life-changing event, reaching out to track down old friends from a happier time. Jim remembered coming to the game with Dick and Paul and when he brought it up, my immediate reaction was a total recall of my lousy pitching performance. Funny thing: all Jim remembered was that I hit a home run. Go figure.

Dick saw me throw the fifth and final no-hitter of my "career" when I was thirteen. After that, things kind of went downhill. That's right: I peaked at thirteen. Nonetheless, he remained a loyal fan to the end and wound up following our American Legion team for two summers when I was sixteen and seventeen. That was probably the most fun I had with my brother as a baseball fan.

Stan McWilliams was our legion coach and he'd had a pretty decent run as a professional ballplayer, playing in the Boston Red Sox organization. Stan had an intricate system of offensive signs that he taught us and he'd change them a little for each game. One day I was explaining the signs to Dick and he got very excited and made me promise to go over them with him before every game. So, right before the start of a game, I'd meet Dick down by the bullpen and give him the signs. During the game, if Stan put on a play—a bunt, or hit-and-run, or steal, or squeeze, or whatever—I'd look up in the stands and see my brother elbowing the person sitting next to him because he knew what was coming. He absolutely loved being into the game.

After my playing days were over, Dick had the opportunity to follow his stepson, Richard Rodas, who was an accomplished left-handed pitcher. Rich signed a contract with the Dodgers, came up through the organization and eventually made the big club. It looked like Rich would have a fine major league career until he injured his pitching shoulder while running the bases. He never fully recovered from the injury. But during his climb through the Dodger system, Dick and Monica traveled far and wide to watch him play. Tommy Lasorda was the Dodger manager in those days and I've often wondered if Rich ever gave my brother Tommy's signs.

So that was our baseball connection. From Dick's playing days in sandlot ball to Little League tournaments up and down the Central Valley to American Legion games down at good old Wilson Park in Vallejo. From Mr. Boyle to Stan McWilliams to Tommy Lasorda. No matter how you slice it, that's a lot of hot dogs.

A Christmas kiss to remember...

Winter vacation was one of my favorite times of the year. Two full weeks with no school, lots of basketball to be played, and the holiday season in full swing. It was always a special time at our house in Vallejo. My Mom would be baking up a storm in the kitchen, making fruitcakes to send to all of our relatives. The house would be filled with the aroma of baking apples and walnuts and candied fruit and spices. I'm sure that there were cousins out there that had a small stack of fruitcakes from years past, reluctant to throw them out, and even more reluctant to eat them. Fruitcake is an acquired taste. I, for one, loved my mother's fruitcake, especially when it was still warm from the oven. No wonder I was a chubby little kid.

The smell of a fresh juicy orange is another thing I associate with winter vacation. Every year, a rancher from the Napa Valley would call and take our order for tree ripened navel oranges, which he would deliver by the case. I've never tasted better oranges. We'd go through a case in nothing flat, most of them consumed by me.

Then of course, there was my Dad and his homemade Tom 'n Jerrys. He'd whip up a batch or two during the holidays and fill the kitchen with the smell of cinnamon, clove, and nutmeg, not to mention the rum and brandy. It's a strange thing, but every time I get a whiff of those spices I'm suddenly a kid again, back in the old house on Russell Street. I still have my Dad's special Tom 'n Jerry mugs. And I still remember the recipe!

One winter vacation—I think I was about fourteen—I was coming home from playing basketball with my friends and I noticed my Mom's car was gone. My bedroom had been added on to the house and I had my own private door off the patio in back. As I went around past the garage to let myself in, I heard my dog George prancing and whining, anxious to be let into the warm house from the cold garage. I let myself in, tossed my jacket on the bed and went to see who was at home. As I entered the living room, there was Dick stretched out on the couch, a pillow tucked under his head, sound asleep. The lights of the Christmas tree were on and he was thoroughly enjoying a cozy afternoon nap. I knew right away what I had to do.

I went through the kitchen and opened the door to the garage and let George in. I quickly removed his collar so that his license tags wouldn't jingle and wake my brother. Then I led George into the living room and pointed to Bro. Dick. George was so happy to see him! He went into a full-body wag and trotted over to the couch where he promptly stuck his ice-cold nose in Dick's face and gave him a big slurpy kiss. I swear my brother elevated three feet off the couch, and then let fly a stream of expletives that sent George running for cover. Then Dick saw me standing there, laughing so hard I nearly wet my pants. Now the expletives were flying at me, which only made me laugh harder. After a minute or so, Dick was laughing just as hard as I was. It took George a little longer to recover.

Winter vacation was always special—the sights, the sounds, the smells—but this was one that I'll never forget. It is a wonderful gift when you can laugh at yourself. My brother had that gift in spades.

Please come to the front desk...

There was always a dance at the high school on Saturday night. It would be in the women's gym and it was the place to be for all of us guys who were unattached. You could catch up on all the gossip with your friends and maybe a girl you liked would be there to flirt with. You might even dance a little. That's where I was one Saturday in October during my sophomore year when a woman's voice suddenly crackled over the PA system: "Charlie Spooner, please come to the front desk. Charlie Spooner, to the front desk."

The front desk was actually a small table just inside the entrance to the gym where a couple of adult chaperones were stationed to check student body cards and sell tickets to the dance. I walked out of the gym and down the long hall that led to the entrance, and then I saw my brother standing there, obviously very tense and agitated.

"Something's happened," he said. "You have to come with me." He obviously did not want to say more than that until we were outside. As we walked out of the gym, I looked to him for an explanation. "You'd better brace yourself, Charlie. Daddy had a heart attack," he said. "He's dead." That stopped me in my tracks for a few seconds while I caught my breath. Then we headed on to the car in silence.

I was shocked but not surprised. We all knew Dad was very sick, that he'd suffered a stroke months earlier, and that the doctor had said there was little he could do to help him. Later I would learn that he had been diagnosed with advanced "hardening of the arteries" and had been told to go home and put his affairs in order. As I sit here fingering the scar on my chest from my own five-way bypass, I wonder if my father would have been a candidate for heart surgery, if it would have added years to his life? He was in his early sixties, younger than I am now, but there was no such thing as bypass surgery at that time.

My Dad was a fighter and he fought back against that initial diagnosis. He went on a strict low-fat, low-sodium diet and his weight went from 225 to 180 lbs. He'd been a heavy smoker his entire life—cigarettes, cigars, and a pipe—but he quit cold turkey. When he went on disability leave from the shipyard, he began to take long walks with our dog George, and friends would report seeing him miles from home with George trotting along beside him on a leash. Certainly all this discipline and exercise prolonged his life, but it was already too late. First came the stroke that left his right side slightly impaired, and now the massive heart attack that his doctor had predicted.

On the drive home, Dick filled me in on what had happened. Dad had gone into the bathroom not long after I left for the dance with my friends. They heard a loud crash as he fell against the bathroom door and when he didn't respond, Dick had to force the door open to get inside. In the meantime, Mom called the doctor who said he would be there as soon as possible. That's right: they still made house calls in those days.

When the doctor arrived, he examined my father and then came into the dining room where Dick was trying to keep Mom calm. He said, "Well, he's gone." Just like that. This of course sent Mom into hysterics and it was several minutes before my brother could calm her again. Dick alerted our sister Edna in San Francisco, and then called Wiggin's Funeral Home, a long established business in town, to arrange for the body to be picked up. He called a neighbor to stay with Mom and then hurried to the high school to collect me.

We arrived at home just a few minutes ahead of the men from the funeral home. They came into the house with a gurney, carefully extricated my father's body from the bathroom (no easy task, given the tight quarters), and then prepared to leave. I will never forget the scene that followed as Mom clutched and tried to hold on, wailing her grief as they took my father away. Again, it fell to my brother to hold her back and contain her hysteria.

Shortly after that, the house began to fill with friends and family, most of them carrying hastily prepared meals and snacks and desserts. I slipped away into the garage to keep George company. As I scratched his ears and accepted his wet kisses, I thought of all the miles he had logged with Dad and wondered if he would miss him too.

I didn't cry, at least not then. That would come later. My feelings for my father were very complex and jumbled. We had been inseparable when I was little and, except for work, he took me everywhere he went, including all of his favorite saloons. It was a time when no one thought twice about a little boy tagging along with his dad to the neighborhood pub. Dad started playing catch with me in the backyard when I was only three and he was my bullpen catcher as I grew up, constantly helping me to refine my skills. He wasn't one to say *I love you*; his generation wasn't like that. But I knew he loved me and was proud of me. Deep down, I loved him too.

Things were not always rosy between my father and me. From the age of eight or nine, I found that I was angry with him much of time. For one thing, I thought he was too hard on my mother. For another, he'd had a falling out with my sister and refused to speak to her. Which meant that he never spent time with Audrey, his only grandchild. Which meant that my Mom and I had to sneak away to San Francisco for visits, careful to get back to Vallejo before my father came home from work. I was angry that he could not reach out and forgive and pull our family together again.

When he got sick, and especially when he suffered his stroke, I was thoroughly confused and upset by his behavior. This man who had been a tower of strength—the strongest, hardest-working man I've ever known—was suddenly afraid and clingy and depressed. I just couldn't deal with it. I wanted him back the way he was, the way he'd always been, warts and all.

In the weeks and months that followed Dad's death, we all came to appreciate the load he had carried in our lives. Taking care of the house, and the yard, and his vegetable garden, and the car, and seeing to it that bills were paid on time, and that we had everything we needed. Now almost all of that fell on my brother. Mom and I looked to Dick for everything. When something broke, Dick got it fixed. When an extraordinary bill came due, he and my sister Edna took care of it. The family made a conscious decision to shelter me from all of this, especially from any worries about money. But I heard enough and understood enough to know that it was a constant concern. Through it all, I can honestly say that I never wanted for anything.

So, our physical needs were taken care of. That was only part of the equation. Our mother was an emotional basket case, completely cut adrift by her husband's death. And I was sixteen, itching to break out and let my long-suppressed wild child run free. My brother had all of that to deal with as well.

I'm sure that Edna and Dick had to sacrifice to hold things together for Mom and me, and I'm sure that meant deferring dreams of their own. I know my brother had to defer his share. Dreams like returning to college to finish his degree, or building a little ski cabin in the Sierras. Simple little dreams like having your weekends free to hang out with your friends and do whatever you wanted to do. Instead, he chose to be there for us, coming home nearly every weekend from Sacramento.

Think about this: my brother was only twenty-five years old! How many twenty-five year-olds do you know who are willing and able to handle that kind of responsibility? We were blessed to have him in our lives.

The funniest guy in the world...

Dick loved to laugh. He had a great little cackle that sort of took over his whole body. If you want to know what it was like, just listen and watch my daughter Kim laugh. Almost a carbon copy of her uncle! Kim darlin', don't ever change that laugh. It brings back great memories.

During the fifties and sixties, if you had a pulse and you had access to a TV, you watched the Ed Sullivan Show on Sunday nights. It was the prototype variety show and it brought a cross-section of the world of entertainment into our living rooms. My brother and I loved the comedians. It was the Ed Sullivan Show that introduced us to Jack Carter, Jackie Mason, Jackie Leonard and Shelley Berman. Then came Woody Allen, Richard Prior, George Carlin, Bob Newhart, and a very young Bill Cosby. There were the great veterans like Myron Cohen and Henny Youngman. And don't forget the comedy teams: Martin & Lewis, Stiller & Meara, Burns & Schriber, Rowan & Martin. The list goes on and on. Of course the historic shows featuring Elvis and Beatles were fun to watch, but that was icing on the cake. We were there for the comedians, and Ed never disappointed us.

As time went on, I came to realize that I, too, could make my brother laugh. He was a great audience. I'd bounce sarcastic remarks or pointed one-liners off of him and he would crack up. Of course, he'd bounce them right back at me. Some of them were classics. For example, we were driving one day and singing along with the radio. The song ended and Dick hit me with this one:

"Charlie, what did you do with the money?"

I said, "What money?"

"The money Mom gave you for singing lessons."

Another example: I was going through the proofs for my senior picture and came across one I liked. I showed it to Dick and said, "How's this? Kinda looks like Frank Sinatra." He came back with, "I'd say it's more like 'Bugetta Kills Snails.'" I went ahead and selected that shot for the yearbook, but I've always thought of it as the Bugetta picture.

The net effect of all this was that when we were hanging out together, we kept each other in stitches most of time. My friends would join in the fun and we'd have Dick cackling all day long.

One weekend, Dick brought a girl home with him. Her name was Glenda and they'd been dating for a while. We all had a hard time seeing the attraction because even though Glenda was kind of cute, she was a biker chick through and through. I don't remember any tattoos, but I wouldn't have been surprised. Anyway, we decided to take a drive to Stinson Beach on Saturday. My friend Bruce Bigelow came along for the ride. On the way, we started quizzing Glenda about motorcycles and she gave us a rundown of her favorites: Harley-Davidson, BSA, Triumph, and so on. As she ticked them off, I would come up with a one-liner poking fun at the name. BSA stood for "Better Stay Auf." TR (Triumph) was "Try 'n Ride it." H-D (Harley) was "Hardly-Drivable." And so it went. My brother was cracking up and after a while, Glenda got into the spirit of the thing. Finally, she turned to my brother and said, "Now I see why you go home to Vallejo all the time."

It was a nice compliment and it only reinforced my opinion: with my brother around, I was the funniest guy in the world.

Weekend warriors...

I went to a play recently. It was the Sacramento Theater Company's production of Steinbeck's *Of Mice and Men*. There was no curtain to raise for the opening scene. Instead, the houselights dimmed to black, the stage lights came up, and George and Lenny entered stage left.

That's sort of what it was like for Mom and me when we knew Dick was coming home for the weekend. On Thursday after school, I would go into what wife Barbara calls my Suzy Homemaker routine: vacuuming, dusting, scrubbing the bathroom and mopping floors. Mom would make a long list and head off to the commissary on the shipyard to shop for the weekend. She'd stock the house with fruits and veggies, snacks and drinks, and all the fixings for a special Sunday dinner. By the time Friday evening rolled around, the house was in tip-top shape and the cupboards and fridge filled to overflowing.

My brother would arrive from Sacramento around 7:00 p.m. Mom and I would be sitting in the living room, trying to act nonchalant, but glancing out the window every minute or so to see if he was safely home. Dick would come up the walk and into the house, and then it was like the stage lights coming up: our weekend could begin.

Through the daylight saving months, he'd drop his bag in his room, grab a cold Hamm's from the fridge, and we'd go outside to inspect the yard. Landscaping became our ongoing project after our father died. Dad had kept about three quarters of the backyard for his vegetable garden and there was no way Dick and I were going to maintain that tradition. So we planted grass, which came up thick and green, a tribute to the thousands of yards of steer manure Dad had worked into the soil over the years. We built brick planters around the foundation at the back of the house and filled them with exotic plants from the Vallejo Nursery over on Springs Road. We kept some flowerbeds for annuals and rotated them according to the season. As I said, it was our project.

The purpose of the Friday night inspection was to see how things were going and to map out the work that needed to be done. Saturday was generally devoted to yard work: mowing, trimming, pruning and planting. One favorite thing to do was to cruise over to the nursery and browse through the rows of trees and shrubs and flowers. We tried lots of things that didn't work out, but it never dimmed our enthusiasm. I have to say that we kept the place looking pretty spiffy. And we had pet names for our favorite plants. A fruitless mulberry tree became a *mulless fruitberry*. We couldn't remember the name of one of the plants, but the tag on it said "prune heavily," so we just called it the *prune heavily*. You get the picture.

I would go out with my friends on Saturday night, to a movie or bowling or a dance at the High School. Dick occasionally had a date with a girl in town named Laurie. She was very pretty and the family got its hopes up that this would be the girl, but I don't think it ever went beyond casual dating.

We'd wind up back at the house around midnight and then the fun would begin. We'd hustle over to a place called Red's on Solano Avenue to pick up a pizza and then gather around the table in our dining room. My friends Dillon Mini, Bruce Bigelow, and Jim Decious would join us. Mom always had something fresh-baked for us to chase down the pizza. Then we'd clear the table, break out the Tripoli board and launch into a spirited game. Tripoli is a board game that I guess can be described as part poker and part gin rummy. Anyway, the game would rage on until 2:00 or 3:00 a.m.

I'd take a break from the game at times and go into my bedroom, which was right off the dining room. I'd turn on the radio real low and pick up an all-night jazz station out of the Bay Area. But I always left the door open. It gave me a good feeling to see and hear my mom, my brother, and my friends talking and laughing and having a good time, with Dizzy Gillespie or Gerry Mulligan & Chet Baker providing the sound track.

A typical Sunday involved going over to the high school courts to play hours and hours of tennis. Usually this was just Dick and Bruce and I, but sometime the other guys would join us. My brother was a good tennis player, gliding around the court with that long stride of his. In fact, we were all pretty evenly matched which made for good competition.

After tennis, we would head home to shower and clean up in time for Sunday dinner. Mom's specialty was a sirloin tip roast with mashed potatoes, pan gravy, lots of fresh veggies, and chocolate devil's food cake for desert. After that we'd collapse in the front room and wait for the Ed Sullivan Show to start.

That was a typical weekend with the Spooners.

When Ed Sullivan said goodnight, it was time for Dick to pack his car and head back to Sacramento, and time for me head for my desk and make a half-hearted attempt to do the homework I'd been putting off all weekend. As he left the house and went down the walk to his car, it was like the stage lights dimming in the theater. For Mom and me, it wouldn't be as bright again until the next time he came home.

A long way back to the top...

I don't know precisely when Dick discovered skiing, but I do know where. It was at Strawberry up on Highway 50. I know this because he immediately stuck a picture postcard of Strawberry Lodge in the corner of the mirror in his bedroom, right across from the picture of Teresa Brewer, his ideal woman. I doubt that they still have an operating ski lift at Strawberry, but the lodge with its gables all along the front roofline is still there. It didn't take long for my brother to figure out that there were far better places to ski, resorts like the old Sierra Ski Ranch and Sugar Bowl, or Alpine Meadows and Heavenly Valley. He was hooked.

We should have saved his first set of skis because they would be considered antiques today. They were made of wood—I think it was hard maple—and the bindings were a lever and cable contraption where the cable wrapped around a deep groove in the heel of your boot. It was amazing that anyone could ski with this equipment and not end up with knee surgery.

As technology progressed, Dick upgraded his equipment and spent all the time he possibly could on the ski slopes. He once told me that when the snow was good, the weather decent, and the crowds small, skiing was the purest form of fun. Experience taught me that he was right.

I had my first taste of skiing on the bunny hill at Heavenly Valley with my friend Dillon Mini. He had tried it a few times and told me that all I had to do was bend my knees, lean forward a little, and try not to fall down. And that's exactly what I did, zooming from the top of the lift to the bottom in a perfectly straight line. No one said anything about turning.

I've never taken a lesson, but when I started tagging along with Dick, he took me aside at the bottom of the hill and gave me a few pointers on some fundamentals, like side stepping, and snowplowing, and how to make basic turns. Then he took me up to the top of the hill and said, "Just follow me and do what I do." My brother was a smooth, controlled, elegant skier. He made it look easy. It seemed like he was always in control and I can't remember him taking a bad fall, though I'm sure it happened. I did my best to keep up with him.

Our favorite place to ski was Heavenly Valley. The hill is so massive and the view from the top of the main lift is breathtaking. We never tried to ski the face, mainly because I wasn't up for it, but there were numerous trails to take from the top that provided all the challenge we needed. The great thing about Heavenly as far as I was concerned was that you spent most of your time on the hill and less time in line for the lift. It could take a half hour or more to ski all the way down from the top before you had to queue up for the lift.

I have to confess that we got into the habit of doing something that is a no-no. We'd drop down off the groomed ski run and blaze trails down through the trees and the virgin snow. More than once we got ourselves way down into a canyon and had to come sidestepping back up to the main trail. Dangerous stuff, but man was it fun.

We were skiing at Heavenly one very clear cold day and after several runs down the mountain, we went into the warming hut at the top of the main chairlift to thaw out for a few minutes. We ordered cups of steaming hot chocolate and sat down at a table next to a window on the west side of the hut. The afternoon sun was streaming through the window and the chocolate was delicious and before I knew it, I felt my eyes growing heavy. I looked across the table at Dick and he was nodding off too. He grinned at me and motioned toward the door. We finished our chocolate and headed back out to the mountain. If we'd stayed there another five minutes, we'd have been sound asleep. That was nearly fifty years ago, and I can still see my brother sitting across the table from me in that warming hut. It was one of the best days ever.

Dick had a couple of dreams, all wrapped around his love of skiing. The first was to finish his bachelor's degree and I think he lacked about sixty units to reach that goal. He worked out a plan to attend the University of Utah in Salt Lake City where he could live with our Aunt Teresa and Uncle Dude. Aunt Teresa adored my brother and was excited to have him stay with their family. The skiing tie-in was the magnificent powder snow at resorts nearby such as Alta. For my brother, it was like going to school in paradise. Unfortunately, he could never convince the good folks of Utah that he was a resident and the out-of-state tuition was a deal breaker. He completed one year at Utah and then returned to California.

The other dream was to have a neat little A-frame ski cabin somewhere in the Sierras. In the mid-sixties, my brother got really close to realizing this one. He bought a lot at a newly developed ski resort called Bear Valley and started pouring over plans and architectural drawings. We even took a late summer trip to Bear Valley to check out the site. Some of Dick's friends from work came along and we camped at a lake near the resort. On one of the days we were there, we found ourselves standing at the top of what would be the main chair lift and we decided to hike all the way down the hill that would be the primary ski run. As we started down the trail, there was a neat little sign that said, "It's a long way back to the top." We just laughed and went on.

If memory serves, it took about a half hour to get to the bottom of the hill, and about two hours to work our way back up. The sign wasn't kidding. When we got back to the top, Dick popped the trunk of the car and unloaded what he liked to refer to as a skier's lunch. He had packed salami and crackers and two kinds of cheese. There were grapes and plums and nectarines. There was a cooler filled with ice-cold soft drinks and beer. And, of course, Mom had sent along homemade chocolate chip cookies. I swear food never tasted so good.

Dreams have a way of changing. My brother never did build that cabin and he wound up selling the lot, but it was a sweet dream while it lasted. Our cousin Margie is an accomplished artist and Dick asked her to paint a picture of the Bear Valley ski run from photos he had taken. That oil-on-canvass hung on the wall of his home for many years. I'm sure it's still around somewhere. We should have had Margie add that little sign: "It's a long way back to the top."

Adventures in the Green Bug...

Along about 1960, Dick got the sports car bug. He took me along shopping around the area, and he finally decided on an Austin-Healy Sprite from a dealership up in Napa. It was medium green in color and had prominent headlights that stuck up out of the hood, which made it look like a little green bug. It had a ragtop and removable side windows that fastened to the doors. All in all, it was a homely little vehicle, but we loved it to bits. It became the magic carpet that took us in search of adventure.

Of course, one of the first things we had to do was to go out and buy sports car caps. We bought little Ivy League snap-brim numbers that we thought looked real jaunty. We'd cruise down the road and if we saw another sports car coming in the opposite direction, we'd honk the horn and wave. Most of the drivers would honk and wave back, but there were some grizzled veterans that gave us the "stank eye" and went right on by. You could almost hear them saying, "Damn rookies."

When it came time for the Sprite to be serviced, Dick would switch cars with us and, since I didn't have classes every day, I would take the bug up to Napa to the dealership for whatever work had to be done. That meant that I got to drive her for the whole week! I was a freshman at Vallejo JC at that time and I thought I was really hot stuff, cruising around campus in my brother's sports car. What a kick!

The Sprite was definitely a two-seater, but many times we managed to accommodate three by putting some padding over the brake lever and having someone sit in the middle, between the seat backs. Most of the time, that someone was our friend Bruce Bigelow. One favorite thing to do was to head over to Stinson Beach to hang out for the day. Bruce was a great outdoorsman and he would remind us that there was nothing as beautiful in all of nature as a long-legged girl in a bikini walking along Stinson Beach. Repeated research trips proved that he was right.

Another favorite adventure was the camping/fishing/hunting thing. Dick and Bruce and I would zip over to Lake Berryessa, or up to Timber Cove on the Sonoma coast, and camp for the weekend. Bruce liked to bring along his twenty-two caliber rifle and if the fishing wasn't so hot, we'd go hiking through the hills thinning out the ground squirrel and jack rabbit populations. I was a terrible shot, so those critters had little to worry about from me. Or maybe I just couldn't work up much enthusiasm to shoot the fuzzy little varmints. Anyway, that was the "hunting" component.

Bruce really was a great fisherman, and still is. I remember one trip to Berryessa when we set up camp on the Putah Creek arm of the lake. We were up early, fishing along the shoreline and not seeing much action. The sun was just coming up, so Dick and I sat down on the bank to rest and soak up the morning sunshine. Bruce came along and said, "What's the matter? You guys quitting already?" We told him nothing was biting. He said, "Oh, yeah? Watch this. I'm going to put on this Hula Popper and toss it out there by that log sticking out of the water. After it sits for few seconds, I'm gonna pop it once, and then again, and a big old bass is gonna jump out of the water and swallow it whole."

We said, "Yeah, sure. Knock yourself out." Stuff like that. So Bruce tossed that frog-colored popper out there right where he said, let it sit, twitched his rod once to produce a nice "plunk" sound, then twitched it again. The water exploded and a largemouth bass slurped up the popper and the fight was on. Bruce played it nicely, inching it towards shore. It jumped a couple more times and it looked to be about 4 or 5 lbs. Finally the fish was up close to the bank and we could see that the lure was barely hooked through the upper lip. Bruce stepped carefully into the water and reached down to pick up the fish by its lower lip.

The bass gave one last mighty rush, threw the lure and was gone. Dick and I sat there with our mouths open and our hearts racing. Bruce just grinned at us and said, "See?"

How's that for a fish story? And it's all true!

Our last trip together was to Timber Cove, which is one of my favorite places on the planet. The cove itself is beautiful with a nice sandy beach, and there is a creek that runs out of a redwood canyon and out into the surf. It's great to go hiking along the stream up into the canyon. Every bend seems to present a scene more beautiful than the last. I wrote a short story called "The Last Adventure." It's a fictionalized account of that last trip to Timber Cove and I think it's pretty good. You'll have to buy the book when it's published. I'll make sure there is a family discount.

We put a lot of hard miles on the old green bug and towards the end, she was really showing the wear and tear. Dick finally traded her in on a red MGB, a real step up in class. We never got the chance to abuse the new car the way we did the Sprite. That's probably a good thing.

Guess who's coming to dinner...

Dick was our favorite dinner guest, and that statement applies to the whole family. When holidays rolled around, wherever we were gathering—Vallejo, or San Francisco, or Sacramento— Dick would be there. But it didn't have to be a holiday. Any given Sunday would do just fine. I'd call him during the week and if he wasn't doing anything, I'd tell him to come for dinner. It was pretty simple: we relished the pleasure of his company. I especially enjoyed watching Kim and Cheryl climb all over their uncle.

The holiday dinners had a classic component: the Great Debate. The topics were wide-ranging and varied and, let's face it, in the late sixties and early seventies, there was a lot to talk about. There was the war in Vietnam, the ghetto riots at home, the civil rights movement, the assassinations, the violent anti-war protests, and on and on. I would usually get the ball rolling because in those days, I was an idealistic, altruistic, bleeding heart, liberal pain in the ass. And so I'd launch into a rant on the topic of the day and the debate would be on, with Dick and most of the dinner guests doing their best to set me straight.

We had some raging discussions, which wasn't hard to do when you had a protagonist like my brother-in-law Ken. Ken just loved a good argument and he really knew how to push your buttons and keep it going. One Thanksgiving, we got into a discussion of Evelyn Wood Reading Dynamics, of all things. I was working with a guy who had taken the course and became so turned on by it that he talked about little else. He claimed he could read a book as fast as he could turn the pages, and that it was more like seeing a movie than reading. Ken's rebuttal was that the technique yielded little comprehension and zero retention and that Evelyn Wood was scamming the public.

That was Thanksgiving. The next spring, when we gathered for Easter, the topic came up again. This time I stayed out of it. And there was Ken, arguing in favor of Evelyn Wood, using all my arguments. I couldn't believe it! Of course, I called him on it immediately and we all had a good laugh. But Ken's cover was blown: he just loved a good debate and he'd argue either side to keep it lively.

We lost Ken not long ago and I like to think of him now as the captain of God's debate team. Or maybe a supervisor of the handyman squad. He'll be great in either role.

Our cousin Rose worked for KCRA, the radio and TV stations in Sacramento. She introduced Dick to a lady named Dorothy O'Malia who was building a reputation as a psychic in the area. Dorothy had a program on KCRA radio and she was into all aspects of the paranormal—ESP, reincarnation, age regression under hypnosis—you name it and she was into it. Dick really got caught up in it for a while, which led to an unforgettable debate at one of our family gatherings.

Dick made an enthusiastic pitch for Dorothy O'Malia and her psychic abilities and all the weird and wonderful things that were revealed. Ken of course took the position that she was essentially a hack, just trying to make a buck with a slicked-up brand of snake oil. My brother wasn't about to back down and neither was Ken. Finally, Ken pushed the wrong button and Dick had had enough. He announced that he wasn't going to take it anymore, put on his coat and prepared to storm out of the house. He wore a hat during the cold months and as he got ready to leave, he grabbed his hat and pulled it down on his head so hard that it nearly covered his ears and eyebrows. Out he went, slamming the door behind him.

We all felt bad for a while. But typical of my brother, the bad feelings didn't last very long. It wasn't long before we were all back together again, laughing about the whole incident. In fact, I took to doing a spot-on impression of Dick jamming his hat down on his head. It was a hoot and nobody laughed harder than Bro. Dick. I will say this: we never again debated the merits of the paranormal or the talents of Dorothy O'Malia. That topic went into the off-limits file.

I look back on those years and it's clear to me that we were spoiled, and a little selfish. We didn't have to share Dick with anyone. When he and Monica fell in love and got married, suddenly he had a whole new family and a new set of claims to his time. I don't think we took it very well, having to share and not having him around as often. There was certainly less laughter around our collective tables, and the debates weren't nearly as lively.

The good news was that my brother finally found the love of his life. He was the happiest I'd ever known him to be, and that's saying something.

The love of his life...

Dick and Monica worked in the same department for the State of California. That's where they met. I'm pretty sure it was in the 1971 – 72 timeframe when they started dating, fell in love and got married. Monica is a beautiful woman with a great smile and a vivacious personality and I immediately saw the resemblance to Teresa Brewer, even if nobody else did. I think our dad would have liked her. He would have said she was full of P&V.

Monica was a divorced mother of five beautiful children: Richard, David, Lorilei, Jackie and Susan. Richard was the youngest, still in Jr. High at the time, and Susan was the oldest, married and out on her own. They were all great kids and it was fun getting to know them.

Dick and Monica settled into his townhouse in a subdivision called Crosswoods in Citrus Heights. It was a great development carved out of a small forest of oak trees, and their unit had a nice deck that looked out onto a creek lined with more oaks. It was like their own private nature preserve.

Around 1974, they suddenly sold the townhouse and bought a home out in Loomis on three and half acres of land. Before long, there were three horses roaming the property. Actually, I think it was Lori that had the grand passion for horses. Three horses eat a lot of grass, more than three and a half acres can produce, so Dick bought a pickup truck and began making regular trips to the local feed store to buy bales of hay. He owned a cowboy hat that he had picked up while skiing in Jackson Hole, Wyoming, and I'm sure that it came in handy.

Monica tried real hard to get into skiing, but it just wasn't her thing. Instead, they tried square dancing one time with some friends and were instantly hooked. Monica was an accomplished seamstress and she sewed square dance outfits for the two of them and off they went, to events all over Northern California and Nevada.

I forget the year, but Dick decided to take early retirement from his job with the State of California. He and Monica bought a travel trailer and started to take trailer camping trips with their friends.

While all of this was going on, Susan and her husband Ed had a baby boy and named him Keith. Now Dick had someone to call him Papa.

So, that is a brief history of how my brother became a country livin' square dancin' trailer haulin' hay balein' horse rancher. And an honorary grandpa. Life was good.

For me, the best part was seeing Monica and Dick together. It was obvious that they were crazy about each other. I remember a time in the mid-eighties when Dick called one day and said they were coming into Roseville to do some business. We made plans to meet at my office downtown. I was the data processing manager for Roseville Telephone at the time, and this would give me a chance to show them around our administration building and give them a tour of our computer room.

I was looking out the window of my second floor office when I saw them pull into a parking space near the corner of Lincoln and Atlantic streets. They got out of the car and started across the street, laughing, rubbing shoulders, holding hands. I hurried downstairs to meet them and give them the grand tour. After that, we visited in my office for a while and then they were on their way to City Hall, just down the street, to take care of business.

A while later, I was downstairs in the business office when they came walking by on their way back to the car, still holding hands, laughing, nuzzling. Simply put, just two people in love. I started to knock on the window to get their attention, but then decided not to bother them. I watched them walk down the street and I remember thinking, *Good for you, brother! Good for you!*

Just a little spot...

I don't remember the exact date, but I'll never forget the conversation. Dick and Monica told us that he'd seen his doctor recently and had a chest x-ray and that it detected a spot on his lung. He would need more tests but it was probably nothing to worry about. I remember coming away from that meeting thinking *It's only a spot. Just a little spot.*

Of course, it was more than a spot. It was a tumor. Lung cancer. And just like that, my brother was in a fight for his life. His physician referred him to an oncologist and he immediately started a treatment program that included radiation treatments and repeated rounds of chemotherapy. We were hopeful because after all, he was a young man, in his early fifties, active and in reasonably good shape. In the beginning, there was every reason to hope for a good outcome.

In spite of that hope, the diagnosis threw me into a near panic for reasons that are hard to think about and even harder to write about. After being as close as two brothers could be, Dick and I had been distant and removed from one another for about eight years. There are lots of ways to rationalize that fact. Barbara and I were busy raising three little ones, Matt and Rachel, and then Gabe. It was like having triplets! Dick and Monica were very close and involved with her five children, plus their passion for square dancing, and their horses, and now a travel trailer and trips with their good friends.

The truth is that there was something else that divided us like a giant wedge. Dick could have avoided it. I could have avoided it. Neither one of us did what needed to be done. I could even have fixed it after the fact, but I didn't. As my sons like to say, "You'll have to wear that one, Dad." The result was eight lost years.

In one of those famous dining room table debates many years back, the topic was the changes that families and friends go through, how those changes impact relationships, and how people who were very close can ultimately drift apart. My brother said he didn't believe that. He looked straight at me and said, "I know that whatever happens, Charlie and I will always be close." It was as close as he ever came to saying *I love you,* which was just not something we said out loud in those days.

So now I was desperate to make up for lost time, which of course is impossible to do. Still, I had to try. We set a regular day of the week and began to meet for lunch at La Bou on Douglas Boulevard in Roseville. It was close to my office and a reasonable drive for Dick, coming in from Loomis. We met every week for a while, taking our time over lunch, talking about this, that, and the other. Sometimes, when he was in a cycle of chemotherapy, Dick would have to cancel. Just the thought of food made him nauseous. When his hair fell out, he started showing up wearing a little snap-brimmed cap. I think it was a souvenir of a trip he and Monica took to Canada, but it reminded me of the caps we used to wear when we went cruising in the old Sprite. One thing was clear: my brother was losing weight steadily, growing thinner each time we met.

I don't know if the treatment regimen ever made much of a difference. Maybe it slowed down the progress of the disease a little. I know that Monica is a fighter and she urged Dick on, encouraging him to battle as long and as hard as possible. I think my brother saw every "ologist" there is, with the exception of gynecologist, and I have to admit that I became very disillusioned with the medical profession. I came to believe that their last official act would be to remove his wallet, or at least squeeze the last penny out of his insurance company.

Was that a fair assessment? No, of course not. I'm sure the doctors took their cue from Monica and her desire to be as aggressive as possible in fighting Dick's cancer. My attitude came more from my own growing sense of fear and guilt than from anything the doctors did.

Eventually the time came when Dick was too weak to drive, even the few miles into Roseville for lunch. He had entered a whole new phase of the battle. Monica would call, usually early in the morning, and say that Dick had been admitted to the hospital during the night with some sort of crisis, unable to breath, or with severe chest pains, or some other combination of symptoms. Several times he had to be taken there by ambulance. Depending on who was treating him, it would be either Roseville Hospital at the old facility on Sunrise and the freeway, or at American River Hospital in Carmichael.

I would hurry to the hospital as soon as I heard, hoping that it wasn't the final time I'd see my brother alive. There was unfinished business between us and the thought of losing him before it got done was painful. You see, I'd never told my brother that I loved him, and that I understood and appreciated all the sacrifices he'd made to keep Mom and me safe and secure.

By the time I'd arrive at the hospital, Dick would be sitting up in bed or in a wheelchair, looking weak but still ready to flash that brilliant smile at the slightest provocation. The crisis would be averted and the doctors would discharge him and send him home. And I would find myself driving away, that little piece of business still undone, thinking to myself: *He knows that I love him. He must know! After all the time together—talking, laughing, hanging out, digging in the soil, planting, skiing, playing tennis, camping, fishing, hunting, laughing, laughing, laughing—he knows! Doesn't he?*

And then suddenly it was March 5, 1988, and I was rushing to the hospital again, this time for the last time. All my chances to make it right, to make up for lost time and say what needed to be said, were used up. All because of a little spot.

March 5, 1988...

When I arrived at American River Hospital, Monica was there with several of her family members (I can't remember who) watching over my brother. Edna and Ken were on their way from San Francisco and would arrive within the hour.

And there was Dick, looking very tiny in his hospital pajamas, completely bald, his arms tied to the bedrails with cloth restraints. I'm sure he weighed less than 100 pounds. My brother had always taken great pride in his appearance and I was sure he would have been mortified to have people see him like this. Or maybe that was just a random, stupid thought—one of many—that passed through my mind during the course of that day. Appearances really didn't matter a whit.

The day settled into a recurring pattern. Dick's eyelids would flutter and he would begin to wake up; then his eyes would pop wide open and he'd begin to thrash about on the bed, trying to flail his arms and drawing his knees up to his chest. Though his eyes were open, he didn't see us, or at least I don't think he did. Then a nurse would rush into the room and administer a dose of morphine, and very soon he would begin to relax and his eyes would flutter and shut and he'd be at rest again. As the day went on, two things changed: the morphine began to wear off sooner and his breathing became more labored, coming more and more in desperate gasps.

Between these episodes, I had to get out of the room. I found my way down to the end of the hall of the oncology wing where a glass door opened onto a small patio. Outside on the patio, there were generally three or four smokers, lighting up and taking a break. How considerate of the hospital to provide this space where the future cancer patients could relax while visiting the current cancer patients!

I couldn't handle it. I'd hop over the low wall that surrounded the patio and continue out into the parking lot. I wanted to turn around and scream at the people on the patio: "Don't you see what's happening inside to your loved one? Don't you understand the connection? Can't you read the frigging Surgeon General's message on your pack of smokes?

Wake the hell up!" But of course, I was too polite to do that. After a few minutes, I'd head back into the hospital, back to my brother's room.

Later in the day—I think it was late afternoon—the nurse had given Dick yet another dose of morphine and he had shuttered back to sleep, if you could call it sleep. Monica excused herself and said she'd be right back. She was only gone for a few minutes when Dick began to rouse again. I went to one side of the bed and took his right hand and Edna went to the other side and took his left. This time as he came to, it seemed impossible for him to breath. He gasped and gasped again, but it was like there was no air in the room. His eyes were open and staring past us. I heard myself saying, "It's okay, it's okay, just let go, just let go and rest." He took one last gasp and then stopped. And then the light in his eyes changed, as though a switch had been turned off. His body relaxed and we knew he was gone.

Monica and the nurse came rushing back into the room and Edna and I moved away to the end of bed. We held each other for a while and said things that I can't remember. I understood the special relationship Dick and Edna had shared, growing up together, navigating all the twists and turns their lives had taken. She was there the day he was born, and she was holding his hand when he died.

Our mother, God bless her, had been sheltered from all of this, her senile dementia to the point where she barely recognized us when we visited her. We never told her about Dick's death.

After a few minutes, I had to get away again. This time I headed back toward the main lobby of the hospital where I knew there was a small interfaith chapel. When I opened the door, the room was empty. I sat down in one of the pews and let myself go numb. I didn't try to talk to God. That would have been a mistake, given my state of mind. I was angry, flat-out pissed off for everything my brother had had to endure—the pain, the suffering, the nausea, the poking, the prodding, the endless indignities. Nobody deserved that, but especially not my brother who had given so much of himself to his family. If God had started up a conversation at that moment, I'd have told Him (or Her) to go to hell.

I had been there about twenty minutes or so when the door opened and Monica came in. She sat next to me and gave me a hug and we talked quietly for a while. Then she said, "Charlie, Dick was my husband and my lover, but he was your brother. Will you be a speaker at his funeral service?"

I was taken back a little, but then realized that she'd been thinking about this and preparing for it for some time. I choked up at the thought of trying to speak in public for my brother and I told her honestly that I didn't think I could do it. She asked me if I would write something to go into the program that would be distributed at the service. I said that I would.

That was March 5, 1988, the day my brother died. I've thought about it many times, especially about seeing the light go out of his eyes. Funny thing: to this very day, I've never asked Edna if she saw it too.

Afterword...

I sat in the overstuffed chair in our living room with a yellow legal pad in my lap, trying to write my piece for Dick's funeral program. The kids were in the family room watching the Saturday morning cartoon shows and Barbara was at the small table in the kitchen reading the morning paper. I'd start, then stop, then rip off a page and toss it away. There were about a dozen crumpled yellow balls littering the floor. How was I going to get this done? I had to put it in Monica's hands by Sunday at the latest, and at this rate, it wasn't going to happen. It didn't help that I was angry with myself, upset that I didn't have the courage to stand up and speak at my brother's funeral.

I reminded myself of the KISS principle: Keep It Simple, Stupid. Finally, I got something down on paper that made sense. I took it in to show Barbara and after she read it, she looked at me with very wet eyes and nodded.

The next morning, I drove out to Loomis to Dick and Monica's place to deliver my little composition. Monica asked me to stay and listen to the music she had selected for the funeral service. I went into a little hallway just off their family room while she started a tape she had made. There was a window that looked out on their property, out toward the tree line a hundred yards away. A light but steady rain was falling and I stood there while the tape played "Love Story," and "A Love Until the End of Time," and "You Needed Me." That's when the tears finally came, and came and came. Suddenly I couldn't stop crying, and I have to be honest, it felt good to finally let it go.

After the music ended and I composed myself, we visited for a while and I asked Monica if there was anything I could do. She said that Dick loved a flowering quince, the one with the bright red blossoms that seem to burst from the bare branches each spring. She asked if I would pick up one at the nursery. She had a place picked out for me to plant it. A couple of weeks later, I did what she asked. Now every spring when I drive across town, I look for patches of red flowering quince that grow wild along the roadside and it reminds me of Dick. I can see him grabbing a cold Hamm's and heading out to the yard for our weekly inspection.

The quince also reminds me that it is nearly time to go to synagogue and say the Mourner's *Kaddish* for my brother. I know, I know, he wasn't Jewish. I figure it's a lot like chicken soup: it may not cure anything, but it sure can't hurt.

The funeral service on March 10, 1988, was beautiful. Several of Dick's friends rose to say a few words. It turns out my sister Edna wrote something for the program as well. So there we were like bookends wrapped around our brother's vital information.

I thought Edna's piece was beautiful and touching:

> *When a baby grows in the womb it is warm, well fed, happy and content. Then one day it must leave that wonderful place and be born. I remember the day Dick came into this world.*
>
> *Here he grew to be a loving, caring, understanding person. Always giving of himself first. He enjoyed life and all it had to offer.*
>
> *Then came the day when he had to leave this place—a place where he felt the love of family and friends, the warmth of the sun and the green countryside that he loved so dearly—and he was born into yet another place.*
>
> *Here he will find peace and love, contentment and joy. He will leave behind his strength, the love and memories as a dear and loving son, brother, husband, papa, and friend.*
>
> *Goodbye, Dick. Save a place for us in your new world.*

Mine went like this:

> *When I was little, I wanted to tag along everywhere he went and I grew up idolizing my big brother.*

He played many roles in my life. He was my brother, and for a while, he was my father. But more than that, he was the best friend I ever had.

We shared many adventures, and I'll bet we shared a million laughs. I could always make him laugh, make him smile that special smile of his.

So that is what I'll remember most— the shared laughter and the sheer pleasure of his company.

At last, there is a merciful God, and there is a heaven. And now my brother can smile again.

Between the two of us, I think we summed it up pretty well. I hope we got it right about heaven, and I hope we qualify someday. I know my very first words to my brother will be, "I love you."

Acknowledgements

A huge thank you to my wife Barbara for her help with this book, assisting with the selection of the images included in the text, consulting on the cover design, and generally tolerating my endless hours at the keyboard.

Once again I have to thank Harry Diavatis, publisher of the *Monday Update*, for giving me *carte blanche* to post essays, memoirs, poems, short stories, and reviews in his weekly newsletter. I know very few writers with such open, uncensored access to an audience.

And finally, thank you to Casey Dorman and the Lake Forest Writers' Roundtable, and to the South Orange County Writing Critique Group. Together you stoke the fire and make me want to do better.

Printed in the United States
By Bookmasters